W9-BWP-672

Thanks to the following contributors of greeting card ideas and sentiments for this book:

Amanda Dalton
Tonia Davenport
Christine Doyle
Jenny Doyle
Amy Fogelson
Scott Francis
Jessica Gordon
Kelly Anne Grundhauser
Virginia Hobbs
Brian Klems
Steve Koenig
Suzanne Lucas
Vanessa Lyman

Jamie Markle
Kelly Messerly
Greg Nock
Amanda McDaniel Price
Phil Sexton
Jay Staten
Joe Stollenwerk
Rob Strawser
Robert Trachtenberg
Kara Uhl
Holly Yerega
Michael Yerega

... And to the following talented papercrafters for their fabulous designs:

Jessie Baldwin
Linda Beeson
Miki Benedict
Corinne Delis
Christine Doyle
Erin Edelmann

Alecia Ackerman Grimm
Kelly Anne Grundhauser
Caroline Ikeji
Heidi Kinnamon
Stacey Stamitoles
Heather D. White

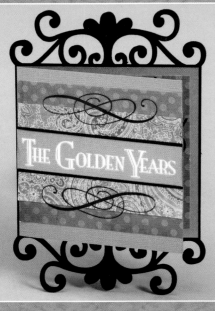

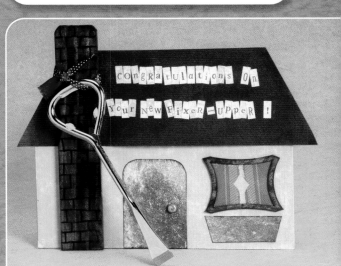

Get Real Greetings

Greetings

creating cards
for your
sassiest
sentiments

edited by Jessica Strawser

NORTH LIGHT BOOKS
Cincinnati, Ohio
www.artistsnetwork.com

Get Real Greetings. Copyright © 2007 by Jessica Strawser. Manufactured in China. All rights reserved. The patterns and drawings in this book are for personal use of the reader. By permission of the author and publisher, they may be either hand-traced or photocopied to make single copies, but under no circumstances may they be resold or republished. It is permissible for the purchaser to make the projects contained herein and sell them at fairs, bazaars and craft shows. No other part of this book may be reproduced in any form or by any electronic or mechanical means including information storage and retrieval systems without permission in writing from the publisher, except by a reviewer, who may quote a brief passage in a review. Published by North Light Books, an imprint of F+W Publications, Inc., 4700 East Galbraith Road, Cincinnati, Ohio 45236. [800] 289-0963. First edition.

11 10 09 08 07   5 4 3 2 1

Library of Congress Cataloging-in-Publication Data
Get real greetings : creating cards for your sassiest sentiments / edited by Jessica Strawser.
    p. cm.
Includes index.
ISBN-13 978-1-60061-001-1 [alk. paper]
ISBN-10: 1-60061-001-3
1. Greeting cards. I. Strawser, Jessica.
TT872.G48 2007
745.594'1--dc22
                2006102896

Distributed in Canada by Fraser Direct
100 Armstrong Avenue
Georgetown, ON, Canada L7G 5S4
Tel: [905] 877-4411

Distributed in the U.K. and Europe by David & Charles
Brunel House, Newton Abbot, Devon, TQ12 4PU, England
Tel: [+44] 1626 323200, Fax: [+44] 1626 323319
E-mail: postmaster@davidandcharles.co.uk

Distributed in Australia by Capricorn Link
P.O. Box 704, South Windsor, NSW 2756 Australia
Tel: [02] 4577-3555

Editor: Jessica Strawser
Designer: Maya Drozdz
Production Coordinator: Greg Nock
Photographers: Tim Grondin; Adam Leigh-Manuell, John Carrico, and Adam Henry of Alias Imaging, LLC
Photo Stylist: Jan Nickum

metric conversion chart

to convert	to	multiply by
Inches	Centimeters	2.54
Centimeters	Inches	0.4
Feet	Centimeters	30.5
Centimeters	Feet	0.03
Yards	Meters	0.9
Meters	Yards	1.1
Sq. Inches	Sq. Centimeters	6.45
Sq. Centimeters	Sq. Inches	0.16
Sq. Feet	Sq. Meters	0.09
Sq. Meters	Sq. Feet	10.8
Sq. Yards	Sq. Meters	0.8
Sq. Meters	Sq. Yards	1.2
Pounds	Kilograms	0.45
Kilograms	Pounds	2.2
Ounces	Grams	28.3
Grams	Ounces	0.035

fw
F+W PUBLICATIONS, INC.

3

4

5

Get Real!

We've all been there: standing in the aisle of a greeting card store, surrounded by sentiments that are too impersonal, too cheesy, or simply not right for the occasion or person we want to honor. The very best cards are often just like your very best girlfriends: one-of-a-kind, fun and sassy, with a knack for showing up when you need them most.

Get Real Greetings is your guide to celebrating your closest friendships with fabulous-looking cards unworthy of being given to anyone else. Making your own cards is fun and easy—all you need are a few simple papercrafting techniques and supplies [turn to page 104 for all the juicy details]—and best of all, it's far more thoughtful than giving store-bought or cookie-cutter greetings. Packed with nearly eighty clever card designs and more than one hundred hilariously real sentiments, this book will have your creative juices flowing in no time. Soon you'll realize that every day you can find a reason to make and give a personalized greeting. Your best girlfriends will be so impressed with your clever creations they'll be begging you to share your secrets!

We'll begin by recognizing those occasions that don't have their own section in the greeting card aisle—but that definitely should! Chapter 1, The Usual Crap, is full of silly sayings in sassy packages to make a friend's day when she calls you to say she burnt her toast, got stuck in a traffic jam, was late for an important meeting with her boss, and is in serious need of a happy hour. If you get a late-night, teary-eyed phone call and you have a friendship emergency on your hands, Chapter 2, Well, That Sucks, has got you covered. Turn to Chapter 3, The Joys of Womanhood, in the event of all of life's estrogen-filled experiences that require some serious female commiseration.

When congratulations are in order—tongue-in-cheek congrats, that is—Chapter 4, Rock On!, is full of the wittiest "best wishes." And the final chapter, Just for [Poking] Fun, challenges you to turn your back forever on boring "Thinking of You" cards by offering plenty of alternative ways to send a laugh (or an eye roll!). Throughout the book you'll also find bonus sections of Surplus Sentiments offering alternate sayings to mix and match with your favorite card designs.

Even better is what this book does *not* have: no sappy five-stanza poems printed on vellum, no photos of kittens wearing birthday hats, and absolutely no cards that you could just as easily give to someone you barely know. *Get real* with these fresh and funny greetings for your closest friends—they'll love you for it!

Chapter 1

The Usual Crap

Warning: If someone asks how your day is going and you're tempted to respond, "Oh, you know, the usual crap ..." then you may be in need of one of these cards. We've all been there: Sitting in our gray cubicles staring longingly at our beach-scene screensavers. Hiding our faces in the grocery store aisles with our two-year-olds screaming at the top of their lungs. Lying miserably on the couch with the flu and nothing to watch but reruns. Don't let your friends wallow in The Usual Crap alone and unappreciated! Share a laugh to let them know that you've been there too—and that sometimes bad days aren't as awful as they seem.

Kelly Anne Grundhauser

supplies

• black chipboard [Trace Industries] • dotted paper [Daisy Bucket] • striped paper [Daisy Bucket] • orange paper • pink ink pad • 2 bracket brads [Around the Block] • large chipboard flower [Trace Industries] • magnifying glass flower [Around the Block] • pink dot stickers [USArtQuest] • 5" [13cm] pink ribbon [May Arts] • font: Quigley Wiggly [Internet download] • ruler • scissors or other cutting tool • glue stick or other adhesive

Cut black chipboard to 5½" × 5½" [14cm × 14cm], dotted paper to 5¼" × 5¼" [13cm × 13cm] and striped paper to 5" × 5" [13cm × 13cm]. Ink the edges of the patterned papers and adhere them in layers on the chipboard as shown. Print the interior text on orange paper, cut it into strips and adhere as shown. Attach the bracket brads around the text. Cut a circle from the dotted paper to fit the chipboard flower and adhere it to the flower. Print the cover text on orange paper, trim and adhere it. Embellish the flower with the magnifying glass flower and the pink dot stickers. Ink the edges of the chipboard flower, then punch a hole in the top of the flower and in the top of the card and tie the two pieces together with pink ribbon.

Had a Bad Day, Huh?

I'm hoping giving you this card means I don't have to hear about it anymore.

it can't be that bad of a day...

the liquor stores are open
and everyone is riding bicycles.

supplies • striped cardstock [Making Memories] • white cardstock • door-patterned paper [Mustard Moon] • white text-weight paper • alphabet stamps [Provo Craft] • black ink pad • red marker • font: Courier New [Microsoft] • ruler • scissors or other cutting tool • bone folder [optional] • glue stick or other adhesive

Jessie Baldwin

Cut striped cardstock to 5½" × 8½" [14cm × 22cm]. Score and fold to create a 4¼" × 5½" [11cm × 14cm] card with the fold at the left. Print the cover text on text-weight paper, trim to 1" × 4¼" [3cm × 11cm] and adhere it to the front panel. Cut a door image from the patterned paper, ink the edges and adhere it to the front panel. Stamp "OPEN" on white cardstock and handwrite "yes, we're" above it with a red marker. Trim around the text, ink the edges with a red marker and adhere it to the door image. Print the interior text on text-weight paper, trim to 1¼" × 4" [3cm × 10cm] and adhere it to the inside panel.

supplies • yellow cardstock • heavily textured yellow paper [Provo Craft] • scribble-patterned paper [fontwerks] • fine-weave mesh [Magic Mesh] • green ink pad • 1 yellow brad [JoAnn] • green silk flower [Prima Marketing, Inc.] • font: Alba Super [Internet download] • lemon template [see page 108] • sewing machine • white thread • ruler • scissors or other cutting tool • bone folder [optional] • glue stick or other adhesive

Cut yellow cardstock to 5" × 12" [13cm × 30cm]. Score and fold at 3½" [9cm] and 9½" [24cm] to create a gatefold card. Adhere a 3" × 4½" [8cm × 11cm] piece of scribble-patterned paper to the left front panel. Print the cover text on yellow cardstock and trim it to 2" × 2½" [5cm × 6cm]. Ink the edges and attach the text to the front left panel of the card by sewing around the edges. Glue a 1¼" × 5" [3cm × 13cm] piece of mesh to the front right panel of the card. Using the template, cut four lemons from the textured yellow paper. Ink the edges of the lemons and glue them to the left edge of the right front panel. Print the interior text on yellow cardstock and trim it to 1½" × 3¾" [4cm × 10cm]. Layer the text on top of a 1¾" × 4" [4cm × 10cm] piece of scribble-patterned paper and attach both to the inside of the card by stitching around the edges. Attach the brad to the silk flower and adhere the flower to the inside panel.

supplies

• dark green cardstock • beige cardstock • light green linen paper • margarita stamp [Art Gone Wild] • brown ink pad • 4" [10cm] green dotted ribbon • variety of markers • 3D gloss medium [Ranger Industries] • glitter • circle hole punch • font: Batik [Internet download] • ruler • scissors or other cutting tool • bone folder [optional] • glue stick or other adhesive

Print the cover text on light green linen paper and cut it to 11" × 4½" [28cm × 11cm]. Score and fold at 3½" [9cm] and at 7½" [19cm] to create a tri-fold 4" × 4½" [10cm × 11cm] card. Glue the bottom and sides of the light green linen paper together to form a pocket, and punch a half-circle at the top. Embellish with ribbon. Print the interior text on beige cardstock and cut it to 3¼" × 5¼" [8cm x 13cm]. Stamp the margarita image and color it with markers. Apply a coat of 3D gloss medium to the image, sprinkle it with glitter, and allow it to dry. Trim around the margarita at the top edge of the cardstock. Adhere beige cardstock to a 3½" × 5½" [9cm x 14cm] piece of dark green cardstock and trim to create a 1/8" [3mm] frame around the beige cardstock. Slip this panel inside the pocket.

Here's a little something to decorate your gray cubicle walls with ...

supplies • green cardstock • red cardstock • pink cardstock • flowered paper [BasicGrey] • striped paper [BasicGrey] • flower brad [Cactus Pink] • 2 silk flowers [Prima Marketing, Inc.] • Velcro circles • 3D-effect pens [Sakura of America] • small zigzag scissors • font: Enviro [Internet download] • ruler • scissors or other cutting tool • bone folder [optional] • glue stick or other adhesive

Cut green cardstock to 4¼" × 12" [11cm × 30cm] and trim one short edge with zigzag scissors. Score and fold at 1½" [4cm] and 6¾" [17cm] from the zigzag edge. Glue a 4¼" × 4" [11cm × 10cm] piece of flowered paper to the larger front flap. Cut striped paper to 1" × 4¼" [3cm × 11cm], trim one edge with zigzag scissors and adhere it to the smaller front flap. Print the cover text on red cardstock and trim it to size. Glue the text to a 1¼" × 4¼" [3cm × 11cm] piece of pink cardstock, decorate both pieces with 3D-effect pens, and attach the sentiment to the large panel. Use a brad to attach the two silk flowers, then adhere them to the short panel. [This card is blank inside.]

Stacey Stamitoles

Jessie Baldwin

supplies
• green cardstock • white cardstock • time card [Acroprint] • alphabet stamps [Provo Craft] • black ink pad • smile sticker • black gel pen • staples • stapler • ruler • scissors or other cutting tool • bone folder [optional] • glue stick or other adhesive

Cut green cardstock to 8¼" × 7" [21cm × 18cm]. Score and fold to create a 4⅛" × 7" [10cm × 18cm] card with the fold at the left. Stamp the cover text onto the time card and ink the edges. Staple the time card to the front panel. Handwrite the interior text on white cardstock and cut to 3¼" × 3½" [8cm × 9cm]. Adhere the text to the inside panel and add the smile sticker.

don't worry...
you're getting
fired soon anyway!

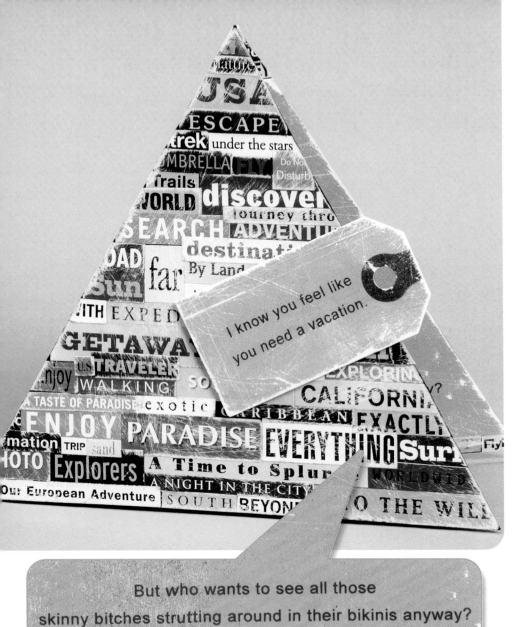

Corinne Delis

supplies • black card-stock • brown paper • small tag [BasicGrey] • stickers [Making Memories] • foam tape • fine-grade sandpaper • font: Arial [Microsoft] • pencil • ruler • scissors or other cutting tool • bone folder [optional] • glue stick or other adhesive

Cut black cardstock to 6¼" × 10½" [16cm × 27cm]. Score and fold to create a 6¼" × 5½" [16cm × 14cm] card with the fold at the left. Measure and mark the center of the right edge of the card and cut from the center point to the opposite corners of the folded edge to form a triangle. Apply the stickers to the front of the card as shown and sand their surfaces lightly to create a distressed look. Print the cover text on brown paper, trim and glue it to the tag. Adhere the completed tag to the front of the card with foam tape. Print the interior text on brown paper, use the card as a template to trim the paper into a triangle, and adhere it to the inside of the card. Apply stickers at the top and bottom of the inside panel, trim them to fit the card and lightly sand their surface.

Stacey Stamitoles

Just think how depressed you'll be when you come back to work!

supplies • red cardstock • turquoise cardstock • flowered paper [Autumn Leaves] • alphabet stickers [Doodlebug Design] • paper trim [Doodlebug Design] • small scallop scissors • large scallop scissors • fonts: Harting, Century Gothic [Microsoft] • ruler • scissors or other cutting tool • bone folder [optional] • glue stick or other adhesive

Cut red cardstock to 8" × 5½" [20cm × 14cm]. Score and fold to create a 4" × 5½" [10cm × 14cm] card with the fold at the top. Cut the bottom edges of the card with large scallop scissors. Trim turquoise cardstock to 3" × 5½" [8cm × 14cm], cut the long edges with small scallop scissors and adhere it to the front panel. Glue a 2½" × 5½" [6cm × 14cm] piece of flowered paper on top of the turquoise cardstock. Trim another piece of turquoise cardstock to 1½" × 5¼" [4cm × 13cm] and adhere to flowered paper. Spell out "vacation?" with alphabet stickers on the front panel. Print the interior text on turquoise cardstock, cut to 2" × 5½" [5cm × 14cm], adhere it to the inside panel and apply the paper trim.

Kelly Anne Grundhauser

supplies • flowered paper [Crate Paper] • striped cardstock [Prism Papers] • variety of alphabet stamps [See Dee's Stamps] • frame stamp [See Dee's Stamps] • brown ink antiquing tool [Around the Block] • clear button • chipboard arrow • light blue cork flower [Prima Marketing, Inc.] • ruler • scissors or other cutting tool • bone folder [optional] • glue stick or other adhesive

Cut flowered paper to 5½" × 11⅜" [14cm × 29cm]. Score and fold at 3½" [9cm], 4" [10cm], and 7¾" [20cm] to create a tri-fold card with a ½" [1cm] spine at the left. Stamp the spine and front edge of the card using the frame stamp and the antiquing ink. Stamp the cover text and ink the edges of the card using the antiquing ink. Adhere the flower and button to the right edge of the front panel. Cut a 3⅜" × 1¾" [9cm × 4cm] piece of striped paper, ink the edges and adhere it to the inside panel. Stamp the interior text inside the card. Ink the chipboard arrow with the antiquing ink and adhere it above the text as shown.

Heidi Kinnamon

supplies • green cardstock • white cardstock • glossy black paper • daisy stamp [Hampton Art] • "Get Well Soon" stamp [Rubber Stampede] • black acrylic paint dabber [Ranger Industries] • text rub-on transfers to spell "You're No Fun..." and "When You're Sick" • 8" [20cm] green gingham ribbon • assorted markers • spray bottle filled with water • ruler • scissors or other cutting tool • bone folder [optional] • glue stick or other adhesive

Cut white cardstock to 8½" × 8½" [22cm × 22cm]. Score and fold to create a 4¼" × 8½" [11cm × 22cm] card with the fold at the left. Cut the edges of the card at a diagonal. Apply acrylic paint to the daisy stamp and spray lightly with water [to soften the stamped image]. Apply the stamp to the front of the card and let dry. Color the stamped image with markers. Apply text rub-ons, the ribbon and the bow as shown. Apply text rub-ons to the inside panel. Stamp "Get Well Soon" on white cardstock and trim it to ¾" × 2½" [2cm × 6cm]. Layer the text onto a ⅞" × 2⅝" [2cm × 7cm] piece of black glossy paper and adhere it to the inside panel. Adhere the card to a 4½" × 8¼" [11cm × 21cm] piece of green cardstock and trim to create a ⅛" [3mm] frame around the card.

When You're Sick

Get Well Soon

You're No Fun...

Get well
and come back
to work soon!

But can I have

your parking space

if you don't?

supplies • green/blue double-sided paper [Around the Block] • green cardstock • red paper [Around the Block] • flowered paper [Around the Block] • large flower brad [Around the Block] • glue dots • font: Vaguely Repulsive [Abstract Fonts] • sewing machine • white thread • ruler • scissors or other cutting tool • bone folder [optional] • glue stick or other adhesive

Miki Benedict

Cut double-sided paper to 5½" × 11" [14cm × 28cm]. Score and fold to create a 5½" × 5½" [14cm × 14cm] card with the fold at the top. Adhere a 5" × 5" [13cm × 13cm] piece of green cardstock to the front panel. Cut 1½" [4cm] squares from the patterned papers and adhere them to the front panel in a grid form. Straight stitch in wavy lines around the edges of the green cardstock and paper squares. Print the cover text on double-sided paper, trim to 2¼" × 2¼" [6cm × 6cm], sew around the text in the same wavy style, and adhere it to the card. Embellish with the brad as shown. Print the interior text on red paper, cut into strips and adhere them to the inside panel by straight stitching their edges.

Heather D. White

'Cause I'm tired of covering for you.

supplies • textured white cardstock • circle-patterned paper [All My Memories] • harlequin-patterned paper [All My Memories] • brown ink pad • 3 matte silver brads [All My Memories] • foam flower [All My Memories] • 6½" [17cm] brown striped ribbon [All My Memories] • tag punch [Stampin' Up] • fonts: Century Gothic [Microsoft]; More Enchanted Prairie Dog [DaFont] • ruler • scissors or other cutting tool • bone folder [optional] • glue stick or other adhesive

Print the interior text on white cardstock and cut to 8¼" × 6½" [21cm × 17cm]. Score and fold to create a 4⅛" × 6½" [10cm × 17cm] card with the fold at the top. Lightly ink the edges of the card. Cut circle-patterned paper to 3" × 6½" [8cm × 17cm], lightly ink the edges and adhere it to the front panel ¼" [6mm] from the top. Print the cover text on white cardstock and use the punch to cut it into a tag. Punch another tag from harlequin-patterned paper and lightly ink the edges of both tags. Adhere the ribbon to the front panel and attach the tags and foam flower over the ribbon. Embellish the bottom right corner with silver brads. Cut the harlequin-patterned paper to 1" × 6½" [3cm × 17cm] and adhere it to the inside panel under the printed text.

supplies • yellow card-stock • striped paper [Fancy Pants Designs] • brown ink pad • flowered brad [Cactus Pink] • brown silk flower [Prima Marketing, Inc] • circle punch • circle cutter • small zigzag scissors • fonts: Kayleigh, Flower Garden [Two Peas in a Bucket] • cosmetic sponge • ruler • scissors or other cutting tool • bone folder [optional] • glue stick or other adhesive

Stacey Stamitoles

Cut yellow cardstock to 4¾" × 9½" [12cm × 24cm]. Score and fold to create a 4¾" × 4¾" [12cm × 12cm] card with the fold at the top. Trim the bottom edge of the front panel with small zigzag scissors and ink the edges of both panels. Cut a 1¾" [4cm] circle at the center of the front panel and ink the edges with a cosmetic sponge. Cut two 1" × 4¾" [3cm × 12cm] pieces of striped paper and adhere them to the front. Print the cover text on yellow cardstock and trim to size. Trim the short edges of the strip with the zigzag scissors, ink the edges and adhere it to the front panel. Print the interior text on the inside panel. Punch a circle from striped paper and adhere it to the inside of the card, aligning the circle with the window. Embellish with the silk flower and brad.

You are so beautiful inside

Congratulations on a successful colonoscopy!

Chapter 2

Well, That Sucks

I think we can all agree that never are we more thankful for our girlfriends than in times of crisis. Sometimes the men in our lives just can't relate to our problems—or worse, sometimes the men in our lives create our problems [or are just not that into us]. We've all had those helpless moments when a friend needs us and we just don't know what to say. The next time a friend calls in a crisis, proceed as usual with the standard emergency kit [red wine, chocolate, tissues and chick flicks]. Then, the next day, or week, or whenever she might just be ready to break out of her rut—and maybe even giggle about it—give her one of these cards. You might say they speak for themselves!

supplies • brown/pink double-sided patterned paper [Scenic Route Paper Co.] • striped paper [Scenic Route Paper Co.] • flowered paper [Scenic Route Paper Co.] • text rub-on transfers [Karen Foster Design, Making Memories] • chipboard brackets [Trace Industries] • alphabet stickers [Scenic Route Paper Co.] • 7 pink buttons • circle hole punch • font: Vintage Typewriter [Internet download] • sewing machine • brown thread • ruler • scissors or other cutting tool • bone folder [optional] • glue stick or other adhesive

Cut double-sided paper to 5½" × 11" [14cm × 28cm]. Score and fold to create a 5½" × 5½" [14cm × 14cm] card with the fold at the top. Trim striped paper to 3¼" × 5½" [8cm × 14cm] and adhere it to the front panel. Zigzag stitch along the top edge of the striped paper. Using the circle punch, cut 7 flowers from the flowered paper. Adhere the flowered circles to the front panel and glue a button at the center of each. Trim the first and last flowers flush with the edges of the card. Spell out the cover text with alphabet stickers and rub-on transfers. Print the interior text on double-sided paper, trim and adhere it to the inside panel. Frame the text with chipboard brackets.

Sorry to hear about your breakup.
Let's have a night out on me!

I just won $300 in the pool.

supplies • white glossy card-stock • glossy black paper • blue linen paper • textured white card-stock • woman with drink stamp [Inky Antics] • black ink pad • 8" [20cm] black ribbon • variety of markers • 3D gloss medium [Ranger Industries] • 1 glue dot • font: Eurostile [Microsoft] • ruler • scissors or other cutting tool • bone folder [optional] • glue stick or other adhesive

Cut glossy white cardstock to 6½" × 12" [17cm × 30cm]. Score and fold to create a 6" × 6½" [15cm × 17cm] card with the fold at the left. Stamp the woman's image onto textured white cardstock and color it with markers. Apply a coat of 3D gloss medium and allow it to dry. Trim the image to 1¾" × 4½" [4cm × 11cm] and adhere it to a 2" × 4¾" [5cm × 12cm] piece of glossy black paper. Print the cover text on blue linen paper, cut to 5½" × 6" [14cm × 15cm], and adhere it to a 5¾" × 6¼" [15cm × 16cm] piece of black glossy paper. Adhere this panel to the front of the card, then adhere the stamped panel as the top layer. Tie black ribbon in a bow, trim the ends and adhere it as shown. Print the interior text on textured white cardstock, trim to ¾" × 2¾" [2cm × 7cm], frame with a 1" × 3" [3cm × 8cm] piece of blue linen paper and adhere to the inside panel.

Linda Beeson

supplies • brown cardstock • white cardstock • large-print flowered paper [My Mind's Eye] • small-print flowered paper [My Mind's Eye] • pink paper [My Mind's Eye] • white text-weight paper • brown ink pad • rhinestone brad [JoAnn] • 3 purple mini brads [Making Memories] • small scallop scissors • large flower punch [EK Success] • small flower punch [EK Success] • font: Blackadder [Internet download] • assorted circle templates [Provo Craft] • sewing machine • brown thread • ruler • scissors or other cutting tool • bone folder [optional] • glue stick or other adhesive

I wish
I could say
I was sorry
you got
dumped...

Cut brown cardstock to 11" × 5½" [28cm × 14cm]. Score and fold to create a 5½" × 5½" [14cm × 14cm] card with the fold at the top. Cut pink paper to 5" × 5" [13cm × 13cm] and adhere it to the front panel. Print the text on white cardstock, trim to 4¾" × 4¾" [12cm × 12cm] and adhere it to pink paper. Using a template, cut a 4" [10cm] circle from the large-print flowered paper with scalloped scissors. Cut concentric rings from this circle using smaller templates. Straight stitch a ring of paper around the text. Glue the scalloped ring to the front of the card. Punch a large flower from the small-print flowered paper, embellish with a rhinestone brad and adhere it as shown. Print the interior text on text-weight paper, trim and adhere the text, a large ring and a small ring to the inside panel. Punch 3 small flowers from the pink paper and attach them to the inside panel with brads.

But now
I have someone
to hang out with on
Saturday nights.

so you're single again...

give me a call if you need any ice cream or batteries.

Kelly Anne Grundhauser

supplies • white cardstock • flowered paper [fontwerks] • pink paper • flower stamp [See Dee's Stamps] • pink ink pad • 3 red brads [JoAnn] • chipboard flower slide [Trace Industries] • 24" [61cm] pink ribbon [May Arts] • decorative corner punch • font: Poornut [Internet download] • ruler • scissors or other cutting tool • bone folder [optional] • glue stick or other adhesive

Cut white cardstock to 8" × 8" [20cm × 20cm]. Score and fold to create a 4" × 8" [10cm × 20cm] card with the fold at the top. Ink the outside edges. Cut flowered paper to 2½" × 7¾" [6cm × 20cm] and adhere it to the front panel. Print the cover text on pink paper and cut to 1½" × 7¾" [4cm × 20cm]. Use the punch to round the top two corners of the pink paper and attach it to the front panel. Wrap the pink ribbon around the front of the card and pull the ends through the flower slide. Glue the flower slide to the front of the card and tie a bow at the center of the slide. Cut a 1¼" × 7¾" [3cm × 20cm] piece of flowered paper and adhere to the inside panel. Print the interior text on pink paper and trim to 1½" × 6¾" [4cm × 17cm]. Stamp the pink paper with flowers, punch the corners, attach the brads and adhere the sentiment to the inside of the card.

Alecia Ackerman Grimm

I guess what happens in Vegas doesn't always stay in Vegas.

supplies • black pre-cut 4¼" × 6" [11cm × 15cm] card [Die Cuts With a View] • red cardstock • dice-patterned paper [Creative Imaginations] • white text-weight paper • silver metallic ink pad • rub-on transfer stitches [Die Cuts With a View] • text rub-on transfers [Doodlebug Design] • font: Times New Roman • ruler • scissors or other cutting tool • bone folder [optional] • glue stick or other adhesive

Cut a heart from red cardstock and tear it in half. Adhere the two heart pieces to a piece of dice-patterned paper, cut around the heart and glue it to the front of the pre-cut card. Apply the text and stitch rub-ons to the front of the card. Print the interior text on text-weight paper and trim to size. Ink the text and a strip of dice-patterned paper and adhere both to the inside of the card diagonally. Trim the ends of the text strip and patterned paper flush with the edges of the card.

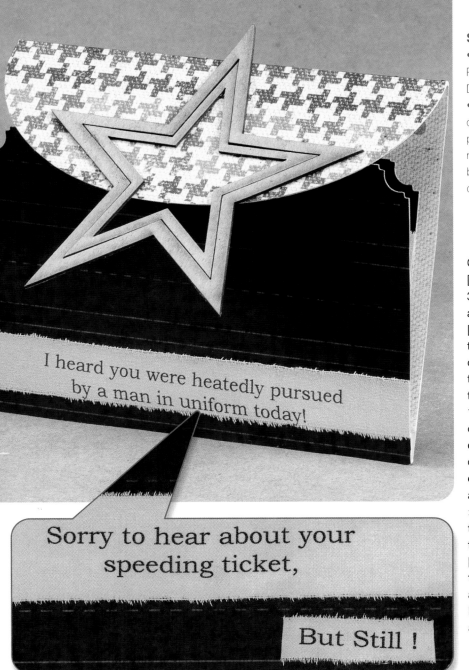

Kelly Anne Grundhauser

supplies • brown cardstock • striped paper [Carson-Dellosa Publishing] • houndstooth paper [Flair Designs] • dotted paper [Flair Designs] • printable cotton [Shortcuts!] • 2 chipboard stars • decorative corner punch • font: Times New Roman • ruler • scissors or other cutting tool • bone folder [optional] • glue stick or other adhesive

Cut brown cardstock to 5⅜" × 9½" [14cm × 24cm]. Score and fold at 3¼" [8cm] and 7½" [19cm] to create a tri-fold card. Adhere a 3¼" × 5⅜" [8cm × 14cm] piece of striped paper to the bottom flap of the card and cut the top corners of the flap with the corner punch. Cut the houndstooth paper to 2" × 5⅜" [5cm × 14cm] and adhere it to the top flap of the card. Cut the top flap of the card into a half circle and adhere the chipboard stars to the flap. Print the cover text on cotton cloth, trim and adhere it. Cut dotted paper to 4¼" × 5⅜" [11cm × 14cm], freehand cut the long edges in waves and attach to the inside panel. Cut a 2½" × 4⅞" [6cm × 12cm] piece of striped paper, trim the corners with the punch and attach it to the inside of the card. Print the interior text on cotton, trim and adhere it to the inside panel.

supplies
• red/dotted double-sided paper [SEI] • yellow paper [SEI] • white cardstock • alphabet stamps [Paper Salon] • arrow stamp [Paper Salon] • variety of colored ink pads • 4 blue brads [Making Memories] • chipboard piece [Making Memories] • corner-rounder punch • foam tape • sandpaper • font: Arial [Microsoft] • banner template [Creative Memories] • ruler • scissors or other cutting tool • bone folder [optional] • glue stick or other adhesive

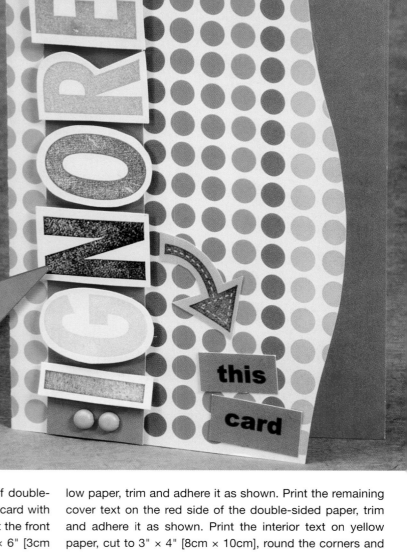

Score and fold a 6" × 9" [15cm × 23cm] piece of double-sided paper to create a 4½" × 6" [11cm × 15cm] card with the fold at the left. Use the banner template to cut the front flap. Attach blue brads to the red side of a 1¼" × 6" [3cm × 15cm] strip of double-sided paper and adhere it to the front flap. Use alphabet stamps to spell "IGNORE" on white cardstock in a variety of ink colors, cut around each letter, and adhere them to the front flap. Stamp an arrow on yellow paper, trim and adhere it as shown. Print the remaining cover text on the red side of the double-sided paper, trim and adhere it as shown. Print the interior text on yellow paper, cut to 3" × 4" [8cm × 10cm], round the corners and attach it to the inside panel. Print "NO Parking" on white cardstock, trim and adhere it to the chipboard. Adhere this to the inside panel. Stamp arrows on the red double-sided paper, trim and adhere them to the interior panel.

supplies • 5" × 7" [13cm × 18cm] file folder [EK Success] • graph paper • 4½" × 5¾" [11cm × 15cm] red envelope [Making Memories] • white cardstock • metal tag [Making Memories] • alphabet stamps [Provo Craft] • black ink pad • silver brad [Making Memories] • black gel pen • ruler • scissors or other cutting tool • bone folder [optional] • glue stick or other adhesive

Sorry you didn't get the promotion...

LOOK ON THE BRIGHT SIDE

I F   Y O U   W E R E   T H E   B O S S,

you wouldn't be able to make fun of the boss!

Jessie Baldwin

Cut graph paper to 3½" × 7" [9cm × 18cm], tear one of the short edges and attach it to the front of the file folder. Adhere the red envelope around the folded edge of the folder. Handwrite the cover text on the metal tag and attach it to the front panel with a brad. Stamp and write the interior text on white cardstock, trim to 3¼" × 3½" [8cm × 9cm], ink the edges and adhere it to the inside panel. Handwrite the remaining text on the folder tab.

supplies
• beige cardstock • green/yellow double-sided paper [Fancy Pants Designs] • striped paper [Fancy Pants Designs] • black ink pad • light purple cork flower [Prima Marketing, Inc.] • stapler • staples • 2 paperclips • font: Dream Orphans [DaFont] • ruler • scissors or other cutting tool • bone folder [optional] • glue stick or other adhesive

Cut double-sided paper to 7" × 8" [18cm × 20cm]. Score and fold to create a 4" × 7" [10cm × 18cm] card with the fold at the left. Ink the outside edges. Adhere a ½" × 7" [1cm × 18cm] strip of beige cardstock with inked edges to the front of the card. Cut striped paper to 2" × 7" [5cm × 18cm], ink the edges and tear one long edge. Staple it to the front panel and embellish with the flower. Print the cover text on the beige cardstock, trim, ink the edges and tear the bottom edge. Adhere the text to the front of the card and embellish with a paperclip. Cut a 3¼" × 3½" [8cm × 9cm] piece of striped paper, ink the edges, tear the bottom edge and adhere it to the inside panel. Print the interior text on beige cardstock, trim, ink the edges and tear the bottom edge. Adhere it to the striped paper and embellish with a paperclip. Staple as shown.

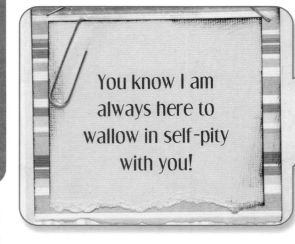

You know I am always here to wallow in self-pity with you!

Sorry to hear you didn't get the promotion

They don't know what they're missing...

The stupid bastards! Sorry you didn't get the job.

supplies • white cardstock • green cardstock • plaid patterned paper [Chatterbox] • woman in party dress stamp [paper candy] • black ink pad • dotted ribbon • button • assorted markers • 3D gloss medium [Ranger Industries] • font: Bradley Hand ITC • ruler • scissors or other cutting tool • bone folder [optional] • glue stick or other adhesive

Cut white cardstock to 10" × 7" [25cm × 18cm]. Score and fold to create a 5" × 7" [13cm × 18cm] card with the fold at the left. Layer a 4½" × 6½" [11cm x 17cm] piece of plaid paper and a 4¾" × 6¾" [12cm x 17cm] piece of green cardstock on the front of the card. Print the cover text on white cardstock and trim to 3½" × 5½" [9cm x 14cm]. Stamp the image onto the cardstock and color it with markers. Apply a coat of 3D gloss medium to the image, and let it dry. Measure and mark the bottom of the white cardstock ½" [1cm] from each side and trim from the marks to the top corners. Adhere the white cardstock to a piece of green cardstock and trim to leave a ⅛" [3mm] frame around the white cardstock. Wrap the ribbon around this piece in a crisscross, embellish with a button, and adhere it to the front panel. Print the interior text on white cardstock, trim, adhere to a piece of green cardstock and trim it to form a ⅛" [3mm] frame around the text. Adhere it to the inside of the card.

Surplus Sentiments

front • I can't believe he
broke up with you...
inside • Stupid bastard.

front • Men just don't understand
how easily manipulated we are with
supportive words and chocolate.
inside • Stupid bastards.

front • So no one told you life was
gonna be this way...
inside • Stupid bastards.

front • What space-saving genius
invented cubicles, anyway?
inside • Stupid bastard.

front • 9 out of 10 mental health
professionals agree that drinking
does not solve problems.
inside • Stupid bastards.

front • I see your hubby sought his
mother's advice in selecting your gift.
inside • Stupid bastard.

front • He's just not that into you.
inside • Stupid bastard.

front • To streamline my Internet dating, I've
been referring my "matches" to a new site
where I think they'd fit in better.
inside • stupidbastards.com

front   Who invented calories?
inside   Stupid bastard.

front   My fiancé agrees that
we shouldn't get a pre-nup.
inside   Stupid bastard!

front   I hear you got married!
inside   Stupid bastard!

front   I can't believe your insurance
company wouldn't cover your breast
augmentation.
inside   Stupid bastards.

front   Ah, happy couples.
inside   Stupid bastards.

front   Somebody dinged
your brand-new car?
inside   Stupid bastard.

front   I hear your ex is getting married.
inside   Stupid bastard.

front   Sorry your husband
forgot your anniversary.
inside   Stupid bastard.

front   Rule #652 of Football Season:
Men will never tire of Fantasy Football.
inside   Stupid bastards.

front   Some people always
look on the bright side.
inside   They are commonly
referred to as stupid bastards.

front   You know what they say:
Once a cheater…
inside   …always a stupid bastard.

front   What can you say about a
gender that's enthralled by boobs?
inside   Stupid bastards.

front   Stupid bastard!
inside   Oddly, it didn't take you long to
realize this card was addressed to you.

front   Friends don't let friends
date stupid bastards.
[blank inside]

front   Most mall parking lots were
obviously designed by men.
inside   Specifically, stupid bastards.

Linda Beeson

supplies • cream/mustard double-sided cardstock [WorldWin Papers] • black cardstock • arch-patterned paper [Paper Salon] • assorted rub-on transfers [BasicGrey, Creative Imaginations] • alphabet stickers [K&Company] • black pen • foam tape • font: Firsthome [Internet download] • ruler • scissors or other cutting tool • bone folder [optional] • glue stick or other adhesive

. . . . IT WOULD TAKE THEM THIS LONG TO FIRE YOU?

Cut the double-sided cardstock to 7½" × 7¼" [19cm × 18cm]. Score and fold to create a 3¾" × 7¼" [10cm × 18cm] card with the fold at the left. Cut a 2" × 10" [5cm × 25cm] strip of arch-patterned paper and tear the strip at approximately 3½" [9cm]. Adhere the long piece of arch-patterned paper to the front of the card and the short piece inside the card. Apply the [10 years!] rub-on transfers to the cream side of a separate piece of double-sided cardstock. Trim around the rub-on and mount it to the black mat. Tear around the edges of the black mat and adhere to the front of the card with a piece of foam tape. Apply the alphabet and flourish rub-ons to the front of the card as shown. Print the interior text on the cream cardstock using the black fill or reverse type setting on your word processing program. Cut around each word, and adhere the sentiment to the inside of the card. Apply the rub-on flourish. Draw dots on the inside and outside of the card with the black pen as shown.

Chapter 3

The Joys of Womanhood

These may not be your grandmother's greeting cards ... but that doesn't mean she wouldn't appreciate them! As women, we possess the unique ability to relate to one another at different phases in our lives based on biology alone—justifiably putting the "moan" in hormones. First comes PMS. Then maybe pregnancy and motherhood—or maybe not. [Either way, you can guarantee people you barely know will ask you inappropriate personal questions about it!] Finally, the worst is yet to come with that word that begins with "men" and ends with hot flashes. This chapter has something for them all—and isn't it about time?

supplies • flowered paper [Cloud 9 Design] • pink tissue paper • printable vellum [Shortcuts!] • glitter rub-on transfers [Cloud 9 Design] • fancy pink brad [Making Memories] • alphabet stickers [Making Memories] • double-sided tape • scalloped scissors • font: Bradley Hand ITC [Internet download] • dress template [see page 106] • sewing machine • thread • ruler • scissors or other cutting tool • bone folder [optional] • glue stick or other adhesive

Score and fold a piece of 5" × 11" [13cm × 28cm] flowered paper to create a 5" × 5½" [13cm × 14cm] card. Use the template to cut the card into a dress shape with the fold at the shoulders. Cut the bottom with the scallop scissors. Pleat tissue paper and adhere it to the sleeves. Attach a ½" [1cm] strip of the flowered paper, solid-side-up, at the waist, and trim it to fit the card. Attach alphabet stickers to spell out the cover text, and straight stitch along the edges of the "belt." Print the interior text on vellum, trim with scallop scissors and attach it to the inside panel. Add rub-ons as shown.

Another bridesmaid dress?

Well, the Halloween Costume dilemma solved for another year.

always a bridesmaid...

sucker

Christine Doyle

supplies • black cardstock • 3 assorted patterned papers • vellum • acrylic flower [Making Memories] • assorted ribbon pieces • black pen • dress template [see page 108] • glitter • ruler • scissors or other cutting tool • bone folder [optional] • glue stick or other adhesive

Cut the black cardstock to 9½" × 8" [24cm × 20cm]. Score and fold to create a 4¾" × 8" [12cm × 20cm] card with the fold at the top. Using the dress template on page 108, cut three dresses from the patterned papers. Adhere the dresses to the front of the card and embellish them with flowers, glitter and ribbon. Handwrite the cover and interior text on vellum and trim around each. Adhere the text to the front and to the inside of the card.

Surplus Sentiments

front   You shouldn't have!
inside   Sucker!

front   You're expecting twins!
inside   Sucker!

front   So you finally got
those season tickets!
inside   ...for the last-place
team in the league. Sucker!

front   Welcome back to the workforce
after all those years at home!
inside   Sucker!

front   Congrats on being
elected PTA president!
inside   SUCKER!

front   Thanks for helping out!
inside   Sucker!

front   Thanks for volunteering to
be the Team Mom this season!
inside   SUCKER!

front   Best of luck chairing
the new committee!
inside   Sucker!

front   Happy Anniversary! You
two couldn't be more deserving
of one another.
inside   Suckers!

front   Congratulations on your
new baby! I know you're looking
forward to a life full of wonderful,
rewarding moments as a parent.
inside   Sucker!

front   Aww! He won you over
with a romantic night out.
inside   Sucker!

front   It's been great working
with you all! It's bittersweet to
be moving on to my next job.
inside   Suckers!

front   Thanks for babysitting!
inside   Sucker!

front   Congratulations on your
marriage! You have vowed to
love one another for eternity.
inside   Suckers!

front   You know, not everyone
can indulge like we do and still
maintain a girlish figure.
inside   Suckers!

front   So you're on a new diet?
inside   Sucker!

front   How's that time-share
working out for you?
inside   Sucker!

Linda Beeson

supplies • pink cardstock • crown-patterned paper [My Mind's Eye] • white text-weight paper • black ink pad • text rub-on transfers [Polar Bear Press] • 2 black rhinestone brads with the prongs removed [Karen Foster Design] • frame transparency [Hambly Screen Prints] • corner-rounder punch • font: CBX-Armymen [Chatterbox] • ruler • scissors or other cutting tool • bone folder [optional] • glue stick or other adhesive

Score and fold a piece of 5½" × 11" [14cm × 28cm] pink cardstock to create a 5½" × 5½" [14cm × 14cm] card. Apply rub-on text to spell "PMS" on the frame transparency, attach the brad heads, and adhere the frame to the card with glue dots hidden by the brad heads. Round the bottom corners of the card with the corner-rounder punch, and ink the inside and outside edges. Trim crown-patterned paper to 4³⁄₁₆" × 4³⁄₁₆" [11cm × 11cm], round the corners, ink the edges and adhere it to the inside panel. Print the interior text onto text-weight paper and cut it out. Lightly ink the edges of the word blocks and adhere them to the inside panel.

46

I don't have pms-

supplies • white cardstock
• light green paper • medium green
paper • striped paper [BasicGrey] •
font: Croobie [Internet download] •
ruler • "double swoosh" card template [Wordsworth] • scissors or other
cutting tool • bone folder [optional] •
glue stick or other adhesive

Follow the card template to cut
the cardstock and other papers.
Adhere both of the green papers
to the front as shown. Print the
cover text on white cardstock, trim
and adhere it as shown. Adhere
the striped paper to the front of
the card, centering the window
over the text. Add a frame of light
green paper around the text window. Print the interior text onto
white cardstock and trim it to size.
Frame the text with a piece of
medium green paper and adhere it
to the inside panel.

I just hate everybody.

Heidi Kinnamon

supplies • yellow cardstock • orange cardstock • light aqua cardstock • waffle-patterned paper [American Crafts] • flowered paper [American Crafts] • alphabet stamps [PSX Design] • text rub-on transfers [American Crafts] • question mark stickers [American Crafts] • 2 2⅝" [7cm] pieces of decorative tape [Heidi Swapp] • 2 clock face transparencies [Heidi Swapp] • cream acrylic paint • paintbrush • ruler • scissors or other cutting tool • bone folder [optional] • glue stick or other adhesive

Paint the backs of the clock face transparencies and let dry. Score and fold a piece of 8½" × 5½" [22cm × 14cm] yellow cardstock to create a 4¼" × 5½" [11cm × 14cm] card with the fold at the top. Trim waffle-patterned paper to 3¾" × 3" [10cm × 8cm] and adhere it to the front panel. Cut out two flowers from the flowered paper and adhere them as shown. Use alphabet stamps and rub-on text to spell out the sentiment on orange and aqua cardstock, trim and adhere it to the card. Embellish with decorative tape. Adhere the clock face transparencies to the front panel and the remaining text blocks and the question mark stickers to the inside panel.

Caroline Ikeji

supplies • pale yellow cardstock • striped paper [KI Memories, Scrapworks] • dotted paper [KI Memories, Scrapworks] • patchwork-patterned paper [Junkitz] • alphabet stickers [Provo Craft] • 3 assorted circle hole punches • ruler • scissors or other cutting tool • bone folder [optional] • glue stick or other adhesive

Score and fold a piece of 8" × 8" [20cm × 20cm] yellow cardstock to create a 4" × 8" [10cm × 20cm] card with the fold at the left. Cut striped paper to 3⅜" × 8" [9cm × 20cm] and adhere it to the front panel. Glue a 2¾" × 8" [7cm × 20cm] piece of dotted paper to the striped paper. Punch three circles from the patchwork paper and glue them to the front of the card, with the smallest circle at the top and the largest at the bottom. Spell out the sentiment with alphabet stickers, following the curves of the circles. Spell out the interior text with alphabet stickers, and frame it with a piece of patchwork paper.

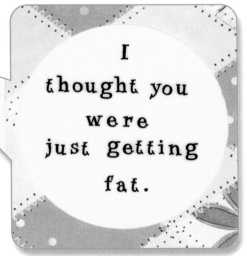

I thought you were just getting fat.

Corinne Delis

It's great to hear you're pregnant!

49

Kelly Anne Grundhauser

You always were

supplies • paisley/teal double-sided paper [Paper Salon] • teal dotted/solid double-sided paper [Paper Salon] • multi-colored dotted paper [Paper Salon] • printable vellum [Shortcuts!] • blue ink pad • 4 rhinestone brads [Imaginisce] • paper flower [Paper Salon] • 20" [51cm] green ribbon [American Crafts] • font: Quigley Wiggly [Internet download] • ruler • scissors or other cutting tool • bone folder [optional] • glue stick or other adhesive

Cut paisley paper to 8¾" × 8¾" [22cm × 22cm]. Starting at any corner, mark the paper 5½" [14cm] from the corner on two adjoining edges. Fold the paper along the diagonal line between these two marks. Repeat this process for each corner to form a card that is 4¾" × 4¾" [12cm × 12cm], with the corners folded down toward the center of the card. Repeat this process again at 2½" [6cm] from each corner and fold the corners back out toward the edges of the card. Cut four 2" × 2" [5cm × 5cm] squares from teal dotted paper and ink the edges of each square. Apply glue to only half of each teal dotted square and adhere to the corners of the paisley paper as shown.

Print "You always were," "Fashionably" and "Late" on vellum and tear out the phrases. Attach the text and rhinestone brads to the teal dotted squares as shown. Cut a 4¼" × 4¼" [11cm × 11cm] piece of the multi-colored dotted paper, ink the edges and adhere it to the inside of the card. Print the interior text on vellum, trim and adhere it to the center dotted square. Cut two strips from the teal dotted paper: one ⅜" × 4¼" [1cm × 11cm] strip and one ⅝" × 4¼" [2cm × 11cm] strip. Adhere these to the inside of the card as shown and embellish with a flower. Cut two ½" [1cm] slits on each side of these strips. Thread the ribbon through the slits and tie in a bow on the front of the folded card.

supplies • purple cardstock • pink cardstock • tan cardstock • white text-weight paper • dotted paper [Paper Salon] • 3 purple mini brads [American Crafts] • 3 yellow paper flowers [American Crafts] • butterfly sticker [Memories Complete] • alphabet stickers [Memories Complete] • black pen • red marker • font: Chinchilla [Internet download] • ruler • scissors or other cutting tool • bone folder [optional] • glue stick or other adhesive

Cut purple cardstock to 8½" × 5½" [22cm × 14cm]. Score and fold to create a 4¼" × 5½" [11cm × 14cm] card with the fold at the left. Trim dotted paper to 2½" × 4" [6cm × 10cm] and adhere it to the front panel. Cut pink cardstock to 3" × 3" [8cm × 8cm], tear one edge and adhere it as shown. Embellish with the butterfly sticker. Spell out "baby" with alphabet stickers on pink cardstock. Print "Having a" and "changes every-thing" in pink on text-weight paper, trim and adhere it to the front of the card. Handwrite the phrases shown onto the tan cardstock, crossing through some with red marker. Trim and adhere the blocks to the front of the card. Embellish with flowers and brads. Print the interior text on text-weight paper, trim and adhere it to the inside panel.

Caroline Ikeji

Having a

BABY

changes everything

diaper bag · sex

sleep · bottles

designer clothes

formula · free time

Including that Pilates body of yours.

I hear you are expecting . . .

. . let's hope the baby fares better than your houseplants

supplies • red cardstock • white cardstock • red/black newsprint-patterned double-sided paper [Creative Imaginations] • newsprint stamp [Stampers Anonymous] • black ink pad • rhinestone brads [Making Memories] • 2 chipboard flowers [Maya Road] • black paint [Plaid Enterprises] • glass finish [Plaid Enterprises] • 8" [20cm] striped ribbon [May Arts] • small scallop scissors • font: Celeste [Internet download] • ruler • scissors or other cutting tool • bone folder [optional] • glue stick or other adhesive

Paint the chipboard flowers with black paint and allow to dry. Then apply a coat of glass finish and allow to dry. Cut red cardstock to 5½" × 11" [14cm × 28cm]. Score and fold to create a 5½" × 5½" [14cm × 14cm] card with the fold at the top. Print the cover text on white cardstock, cut to 5" × 5" [13cm × 13cm] and trim two adjoining sides with small scallop scissors. Randomly stamp the newsprint stamp around the cardstock's edges, then attach it to the front panel. Cut a large photo corner from the newsprint cardstock and attach it to the white cardstock with the black side showing. Place a rhinestone brad in the center of the large chipboard flower and glue the flower and ribbon as shown. Print the interior text on white cardstock, cut around the text to form a heart and ink the edges. Attach strips of newsprint-patterned paper to the inside panel and adhere the heart as shown. Place a brad in the center of the small chipboard flower and adhere it as shown.

Linda Beeson

supplies • yellow cardstock • white cardstock • flowered paper [BasicGrey] • green ink pad • black ink pad • 3 shaped brads [Karen Foster Design] • 2 chipboard flowers [Technique Tuesday] • black gel pen • ruler • scissors or other cutting tool • bone folder [optional] • glue stick or other adhesive

that's a politically correct term for "TINY HOLY TERROR"

CONGRATULATIONS on your precious little blessing!

Cut yellow cardstock to 5½" × 8½" [14cm × 22cm]. Score and fold to create a 4¼" × 5½" [11cm × 14cm] card with the fold at the left. Cut flowered paper to 3½" × 4½" [9cm × 11cm], ink the edges with black ink and adhere it to the front panel. Handwrite the cover text on white cardstock and trim to 3" × 3¼" [8cm × 8cm]. Ink the edges with green ink and adhere it to the front panel. Ink the edges of the chipboard flower with green ink, attach a brad to the center and adhere it as shown. Cut white cardstock to 3¼" × 4¾" [8cm × 12cm], ink the edges with green ink and attach it to the inside panel. Cut flowered paper to 2" × 2¼" [5cm × 6cm], ink the edges with black ink and adhere it to the white cardstock inside the card. Handwrite the interior text on the white cardstock. Ink the edges of the remaining chipboard flower with green ink, attach a brad to the center and adhere it as shown, along with the remaining brad.

supplies • textured white cardstock • circle-patterned paper [Imaginisce] • dotted paper [Imaginisce] • red crosshatched paper [Imaginisce] • 3 mini brads [Imaginisce] • text rub-on transfers [Imaginisce] • assorted rub-on transfer images [Imaginisce] • font: Kindergarten [Mom's Corner for Kids] • sewing machine • white thread • ruler • scissors or other cutting tool • bone folder [optional] • glue stick or other adhesive

Print the interior text on white cardstock and cut to 5" × 10" [13cm × 25cm]. Score and fold to create a 5" × 5" [13cm × 13cm] card with the fold at the left. Cut circle-patterned paper to 4" × 4" [10cm × 10cm] and attach to the front cover by zigzag stitching the edges. Apply the text rub-ons around the border. Cut dotted paper to 2" × 4" [5cm × 10cm], making slightly curved cuts on the long ends. Attach it left of center on the circle-patterned paper by zigzag stitching along the curved sides only. Print the cover text on red paper, trim and glue it to the front panel. Apply flower rub-ons to white cardstock, trim and adhere it as shown. Apply the remaining rub-ons to the front and inside panels. Embellish with 3 mini brads.

u.r. so

hot!

Welcome to menopause.

supplies • textured white cardstock • striped paper [Fancy Pants Designs] • flowered paper [Fancy Pants Designs] • dotted paper [Fancy Pants Designs] • 2 paper tags [Fancy Pants Designs] • text rub-on transfers [Scenic Route Paper Co.] • large red brad [Bazzill Basics] • silk flower [Bazzill Basics] • 3½" [9cm] red ribbon [Fancy Pants Designs] • large chipboard letters [Fancy Pants Designs, Zsiage] • medium chipboard letters [Fancy Pants Designs, Zsiage] • font: Century Gothic [Microsoft] • sewing machine • white thread • ruler • scissors or other cutting tool • bone folder [optional] • glue stick or other adhesive

Print the interior text on white cardstock and cut to 9" × 7" [23cm × 18cm]. Score and fold to create a 4½" × 7" [11cm × 18cm] card with the fold at the top. Cut striped paper to 4¼" × 6¾" [11cm × 17cm] and attach it to the front panel by straight stitching around the edges. Cut flowered paper to 5½" × 3½" [14cm × 9cm], and attach it to striped paper by straight stitching around the edges. Adhere paper tags to the front panel as shown. Attach ribbon from the top tag to the edge of the card, layering it over the edge of the flowered paper. Cover the large chipboard letters spelling "hot!" in dot-patterned paper. Use chipboard letters and text rub-on transfers to spell the cover text. Attach the flower to the card with a brad. Trim dotted paper to 7" × ½" [18cm × 1cm] and glue it to the inside panel. Cut a piece of white cardstock to 4¼" × 6¾" [11cm × 17cm] and adhere it to the inside panel to hide the stitching.

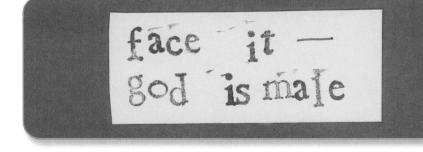

face it —
god is male

Caroline Ikeji

supplies • red cardstock • pink cardstock • blue dotted paper [SEI, KI Memories] • pink dotted paper [SEI, KI Memories] • alphabet stamps [PSX Design] • dark red ink pad • rub-on transfer image [BasicGrey] • 4 matte silver mini brads [American Crafts] • 4 small pink paper flowers [American Crafts] • flower sticker [KI Memories] • foam alphabet stickers [American Crafts] • epoxy alphabet stickers [KI Memories] • journaling sticker [Heidi Swapp] • 3¾" [10cm] black and pink ribbon [American Crafts] • black pen • ruler • scissors or other cutting tool • bone folder [optional] • glue stick or other adhesive

Cut red cardstock to 8½" × 5½" [22cm × 14cm]. Score and fold to create a 4¼" × 5½" [11cm × 14cm] card with the fold at the top. Trim pink dotted paper to 3½" × 3½" [9cm × 9cm] and adhere it to the front panel. Adhere foam letters to spell "MEN" on a 1¾" × 5" [4cm × 13cm] piece of blue dotted paper. Cut blue patterned paper into blocks to separate the letters and apply them as shown. Adhere the journaling sticker, epoxy stickers and ribbon to the front of the card. Adhere the flower sticker as shown and apply the rub-on transfer to its center. Attach paper flowers with the silver brads as shown. Stamp the interior text on pink cardstock, trim and adhere it to the inside panel.

supplies
• white cardstock • heart-patterned paper [KI Memories] • solid pink paper • 2 square die cuts [KI Memories] • 1 round die cut [KI Memories] • black ink pad • tag sticker [KI Memories] • alphabet stickers [KI Memories, Die Cuts with a View] • heart sticker [KI Memories, Die Cuts with a View] • 2¾" [7cm] piece of decorative tape [Heidi Swapp] • 2¾" [7cm] dotted ribbon [American Crafts] • 3 pink buttons • brown marker • ruler • scissors or other cutting tool • bone folder [optional] • glue stick or other adhesive

TWO WORDS:
BIKINI
WAX

SO YOU'RE READY TO start dATInG again...

Cut white cardstock to 8½" × 5½" [22cm × 14cm]. Score and fold to create a ¼" × 5½" [1cm × 14cm] card with the fold at the left. Trim heart-patterned paper to 2½" × 4" [6cm × 10cm] and adhere it to the front panel. Glue the die cuts to the front of the card, layering the pieces. Embellish with buttons. Handwrite the text on the pink paper, trim, ink the edges and adhere the sentiment to the front panel. Apply alphabet stickers to the tag and adhere it, along with the heart sticker, ribbon and decorative tape, to the front of the card. Create the interior text with stickers and handwriting.

You exude the energy of youth!

Who's your plastic surgeon?

supplies • yellow cardstock • white cardstock • paisley-patterned paper [Making Memories] • pink ink pad • yellow ink pad • pink and orange rickrack • pink and clear rhinestones • foam tape • circle hole punch • font: CAC Pinafore [American Greetings Corporation] • flower templates [see page 108] • ruler • scissors or other cutting tool • bone folder [optional] • glue stick or other adhesive

Print the interior text on yellow cardstock, cut to 11½" × 6¼" [29cm × 16cm], score and fold to create a 5¾" × 6¼" [15cm × 16cm] card with the fold at the top and the text inside. Use the large flower template to cut the card into shape. Ink the inside and outside edges with pink ink. Using the small flower template, cut a piece of paisley-patterned paper and adhere it to the front panel. Print the cover text on white cardstock, trim into a circle and ink the edges with yellow ink. Glue the rhinestones to the front of the text piece and the rickrack to the back. Adhere another piece of cardstock to the back of the text piece, sandwiching the rickrack. Adhere it to the front panel with foam dots.

Stacey Stamitoles

Corinne Delis

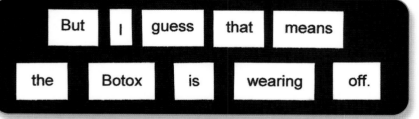

supplies • black cardstock • red cardstock • white cardstock • green/flowered double-sided patterned paper [American Crafts] • blue brad [Queen & Co.] • green anchor [Queen & Co.] • small chipboard letters [cherryArte] • foam tape • font: Arial [Microsoft] • smile templates [see page 106] • ruler • scissors or other cutting tool • bone folder [optional] • glue stick or other adhesive

Cut black cardstock to 6" × 8" [15cm × 20cm]. Score and fold to create a 6" × 4" [15cm × 10cm] card with the fold at the top. Cut double-sided paper to 4" × 3½" [10cm × 9cm] and adhere it to the front panel. Glue a 4" × 1⅝" [10cm × 4cm] piece of the double-sided paper, flowered-side-up, to the front of the card as shown. Print the cover text on white cardstock, cut out each word and adhere the sentiment as shown. Cut out the smile pieces using the templates, assemble the smile and adhere it to the front panel with foam tape. Attach the chipboard letters, anchor and brad to the front of the card. Print the interior text on white cardstock, cut out the words and adhere them as shown.

BEST WiSHES

for a speedy recovery!

NEXT TIME PUT YOUR MOTHER-IN-LAW UP AT A HOTEL.

supplies • textured white cardstock • dotted/orange double-sided paper [American Crafts] • striped/red double-sided paper [American Crafts] • square-patterned paper [American Crafts] • 2 coordinating solid color papers • yellow button • decorative scissors [Provo Craft] • circle hole punch • font: CK Surfer [Creating Keepsakes]; More Enchanted Prairie Dog [DaFont] • ruler • scissors or other cutting tool • bone folder [optional] • glue stick or other adhesive

Cut the double-sided dotted paper to 10" × 5½" [25cm × 14cm]. Score and fold at 3" [8cm] and 7¼" [18cm] to form a tri-fold card that is 4¼" × 5½" [11cm × 14cm]. Using the decorative scissors, cut the tops of the side panels diagonally. Apply glue at the base and flaps of the card to form a pocket. Print the cover text on white cardstock and trim to 10" × 1¾" [25cm × 4cm]. Adhere the text strip to a 10" × 2" [25cm × 5cm] piece of the square-patterned paper and wrap it around the card, adhering it completely. Punch a circle from the red double-sided paper and cut slits in toward the center. Remove two petals and bend and space the remaining petals to create a flower. Attach the flower and button as shown. Print the interior text on white cardstock and trim to 4" × 5" [10cm × 13cm]. Adhere strips of solid and patterned paper to frame the text.

Chapter 4

Rock On!

You're really happy for your friends—you really are! Can you help it if some occasions just happen to be bittersweet by nature? New house, good! Mortgage, bad. Promotion, good! Sixty-hour workweeks, bad. Engagement, good! Marriage … Still good, right? Some occasions are just plain sweet, but that doesn't mean you can't have a little good-humored fun while you help celebrate! Add a splash of sass to your congratulatory sentiments for all occasions, from new years to new jobs to new boyfriends.

supplies • black cardstock • blue paper • green paper • word block stickers [7gypsies] • 2¾" [7cm] striped ribbon [Doodlebug Design] • green rickrack • black pen • orange felt • white felt • yellow felt • 3 yellow buttons • 4 orange buttons • font: Arial [Microsoft] • ruler • scissors or other cutting tool • bone folder [optional] • glue stick or other adhesive

Cut black cardstock to 7¼" × 8" [18cm × 20cm]. Score and fold to create a 7¼" × 4" [18cm × 10cm] card with the fold at the left. Cut blue paper to 3½" × 6" [9cm × 15cm] and adhere to the front of the card. Freehand draw a frame on the blue paper. Print the cover text on green paper, trim and attach it to the front panel. Freehand draw a frame around the text. Glue a 2¼" × 2¾" [6cm × 7cm] piece of orange felt onto the front of the card. Cut a ⅝" × 2¼" [2cm × 6cm] piece of yellow felt and adhere it as shown to create the candle. Draw a wick with the black pen and adhere orange buttons to to create a flame as shown. Cut a ⅜" × 2¼" [1cm × 6cm] strip of white felt, freehand cut a cloud-shape piece of white felt, and adhere both to the orange felt as shown. Embellish with yellow buttons, rickrack and ribbon. Print the interior text on green paper, trim to 1¾" × 4" [4cm × 10cm] and adhere it to the inside panel. Freehand draw a frame on the green paper.

HAPPY BIRTHDAY
YOU don't look A day over 21

I mean, a day over 21 would essentially be 21. You look, like, 40 or something.

Linda Beeson

supplies • flowered/green double-sided paper [Crate Paper] • striped paper [Crate Paper] • yellow cardstock • alphabet tag stickers [EK Success] • word block stickers [EK Success] • liquid glitter [Ranger Industries] • font: Runic Condensed [Internet download] • ruler • scissors or other cutting tool • bone folder [optional] • glue stick or other adhesive

Cut double-sided paper to 7½" × 7¼" [19cm × 18cm]. Score and fold to create a 3¾" × 7¼" [10cm × 18cm] card with the fold at the top. Apply the alphabet and text stickers to spell out the text on the front of the card. Freehand cut candles from striped paper and flames from the yellow cardstock. Apply glitter to the flame pieces and adhere them and the striped paper on the front panel to form the candles. Print the interior text on the green side of the double-sided paper and trim it to size. Adhere the text to the inside of the card, and frame it with thin strips of the striped paper.

supplies • brown/blue double-sided paper [Paper Salon] • dotted paper [Paper Salon] • printable vellum [Shortcuts!] • bird stamp [Paper Salon] • black ink pad • 1 large black brad [Around The Block] • 2 stickers [Paper Salon] • foam tape • corner-rounder punch • font: Mistral [Microsoft] • sewing machine • white thread • ruler • scissors or other cutting tool • bone folder [optional] • glue stick or other adhesive

Cut double-sided paper to 4" × 11¼" [10cm × 29cm]. Score and fold at 5½" [14cm] and at 5¾" [15cm] with the folds at the left. Print the cover and interior text on vellum. Tear the vellum as shown and attach it to a 1½" × 4" [4cm × 10cm] piece of the double-sided paper, blue-side-up. Attach this to the front of the card by straight stitching around the edges. Stamp the bird image on the blue side of the double-sided paper, cut around the image, round three corners, and ink the edges. Embellish with a brad and adhere this piece to the front of the card with a piece of foam tape. Tear the top side of the interior text piece and adhere it to the inside panel. Add a strip of dotted paper and stickers as shown.

Congratulations on your Engagement!

Let me know if you need help revising the "How We Met" story.

supplies • brown/blue double-sided paper [Paper Salon] • red paper [NRN Designs] • 3 coordinating paper tags [Paper Salon] • frame stamp [Paper Salon] • brown ink pad • 4" [10cm] blue and brown ribbon [May Arts] • brown marker • chipboard heart [Making Memories] • corner-rounder punch • font: Lucida Calligraphy [Microsoft] • large heart template [see page 107] • ruler • scissors or other cutting tool • bone folder [optional] • glue stick or other adhesive

Cut double-sided paper to 5½" × 8½" [14cm × 22cm]. Score and fold to create a 4¼" × 5½" [11cm × 14cm] card with the fold at the left. Round the corners. Freehand cut a heart from red paper, ink the edges and adhere to the front panel. Print the cover text onto the blue side of the double-sided paper. Stamp a frame around the text and trim close to the frame. Adhere the text frame to a tag, tie the ribbon to the tag and adhere it to the front of the card. Print the interior text onto the 2 remaining tags and adhere them to the inside panel. Cover the chipboard heart with red paper, ink the edges and adhere it as shown.

She looked at him...
He looked at her...

Everyone who saw

"that look"

wanted to throw up a little.

Congrats
on your
engagement!

supplies

• 5½" × 5½" [14cm x 14cm] embossed card [Die Cuts With a View] • white cardstock • striped paper [Bo-Bunny Press] • heart stamp [Heidi Swapp] • pink ink pad • brown ink pad • gold ink pad • large dotted brad [Bazzill Basics] • silk flower [Bazzill Basics] • text sticker [Bo-Bunny Press] • silver glitter paint [Plaid Enterprises] • chipboard piece [Provo Craft] • sequins [Cartwright's Glitter] • font: Century [Microsoft] • paintbrush • paper towel • ruler • scissors or other cutting tool • bone folder [optional] • glue stick or other adhesive

Heavily distress the front of the card with pink, brown and gold inks. Blend the inks with a crumpled paper towel. Cut striped paper to 4½" × 4½" [11cm × 11cm] and adhere it to the front panel. Stamp the heart image on white cardstock, trim and adhere it to the front of the card. Paint the silk flower with silver glitter paint, attach the brad to the center and adhere the flower as shown. Print the cover text on white cardstock, trim and adhere it to the chipboard piece. Attach the chipboard piece and text sticker to the front of the card. Print the interior text on white cardstock, trim and adhere it to the inside panel. Glue sequins around the text strip.

First weddings are sooooooo cute!!!

Congrats on your new, 2nd career...

I mean...HOUSE!

Stacey Stamitoles

supplies
• dark blue cardstock • light blue cardstock • green paper [BasicGrey] • flowered paper [BasicGrey] • 12" [30cm] blue ribbon [May Arts] • small blue button • oval punch [Marvy Uchida] • zigzag scissors • font: Jayne Print [Internet download] • ruler • scissors or other cutting tool • bone folder [optional] • glue stick or other adhesive

Cut dark blue cardstock to 6" × 8½" [15cm × 22cm]. Score and fold to create a 4¼" × 6" [11cm × 15cm] card with the fold at the top. Adhere a 3½" × 5½" [9cm × 14cm] piece of flowered paper to a 3¾" × 5¾" [10cm × 15cm] piece of green paper. Glue a 6" [15cm] piece of ribbon onto the flowered paper. Adhere this piece to the front of the card, tucking the ends of the ribbon under the green paper. Cut a 3¼" × 3¼" [8cm × 8cm] square of green paper diagonally to form two triangles. Glue one triangle to the front of the card. Print the cover text on light blue cardstock and trim it, using zigzag scissors on three sides. Glue the text and a bow made from the blue ribbon onto the front of the card. Adhere a 3¼" × 2½" [8cm × 6cm] piece of flowered paper to the inside panel. Trim the remaining green triangle with zigzag scissors and adhere it as shown to form the roof of the house. Use assorted pieces of cardstock and green paper to add a door, window and chimney. Glue the small button to the door of the house for a doorknob. Print the interior text onto light blue cardstock, cut into an oval and adhere it as shown.

Kelly Anne Grundhauser

supplies • chipboard mat [Die Cuts With a View] • brown cardstock • striped paper [All My Memories] • brown paper [Around the Block] • printable cotton [Shortcuts!] • brown ink antiquing tool [Around the Block] • 1 green brad • alphabet stickers [Making Memories] • 3½" [9cm] brown ribbon [American Crafts] • black marker • chipboard frame • paint can opener • paint stir stick • glue dots • font: Jenkins v2.0 [Internet download] • ruler • scissors or other cutting tool • glue stick or other adhesive

Heavily sand the chipboard mat with the antiquing tool and cut off the top corners. Cut brown cardstock to 2½" × 7½" [6cm × 19cm] and slope the short edges to form a roof. Attach the roof piece to the chipboard at the left side only. Trim the paint stir stick to your desired height and ink it with the antiquing tool. Using a black marker, draw brick lines onto the stick and adhere it to the front of the card. Spell out the cover text with alphabet stickers as shown. Cut brown paper to form a door and windowbox. Sand the brad, attach it to the door and adhere the door and windowbox to the card. Cut the striped paper to form curtains, ink the chipboard frame and adhere both pieces to the chipboard mat to form a window. Print the interior text on printable cotton, trim and adhere it to the chipboard mat under the brown cardstock. Place a glue dot at the right hand side of the chipboard under the edge of the "roof" to hold the card closed.

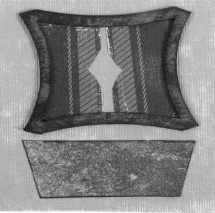

I'll come over and help you work on it
just as soon as I'm up to date on all my shots.

Linda Beeson

congratulations on buying your first house!

just think,
you won't have
to hide the cat
in a pillowcase
every time the
doorbell rings!

supplies • brown/turquoise double-sided patterned paper [Pink Martini Designs] • pink paper • yellow paper • black ink pad • zigzag scissors • font: Jack Frost [Two Peas in a Bucket] • ruler • scissors or other cutting tool • bone folder [optional] • glue stick or other adhesive

Cut double-sided paper to 7½" × 7¼" [19cm × 18cm]. Score and fold to create a 3¾" × 7¼" [10cm × 18cm] card with the fold at the top. Cut small pieces from each of the papers to create a house. Ink the edges of the house pieces. Print the cover text on yellow paper, cut around the text in a banner shape and ink the edges. Attach the banner and house to the front panel. Cut a 3⅜" × 2⅞" [9cm × 7cm] piece of pink paper, ink the edges and adhere it to the inside of the card. Print the interior text on yellow paper, cut around the text with zigzag scissors, ink the edges, and adhere it to the pink paper. Cut a motif from the double-sided paper and attach it to the inside panel.

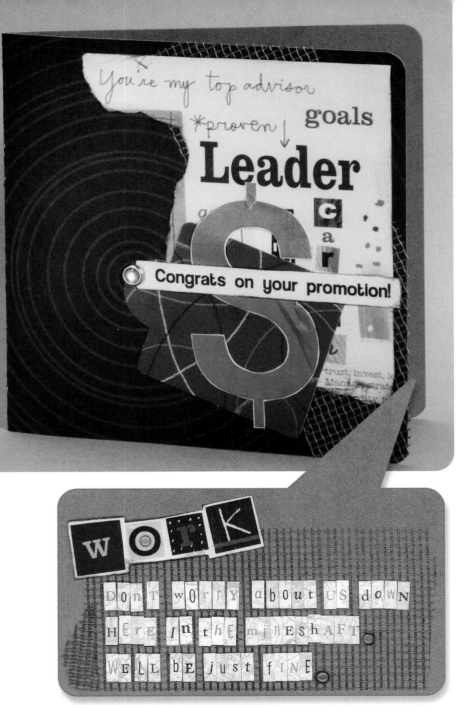

supplies • green/circle-patterned double-sided cardstock [KI Memories] • work-theme patterned paper [KI Memories] • white text-weight paper • gold mesh [Magic Mesh] • paper tag [KI Memories] • gold ink pad • 4 assorted brads [SEI] • alphabet stickers [Making Memories] • corner-rounder punch • bold sans serif font • ruler • scissors or other cutting tool • bone folder [optional] • glue stick or other adhesive

Cut cardstock to 12" × 6" [30cm × 15cm]. Score and fold to create a 6" × 6" [15cm × 15cm] card with the fold at the left. Adhere a 2½" [6cm] wide strip of mesh diagonally across the front panel, trim it to fit the card, and round the card's righthand corners. Cut a 4½" × 5" [11cm × 13cm] piece of patterned paper, tear diagonally, ink the edges and adhere it to the front panel. Print the cover text and a dollar sign onto text-weight paper, trim, ink the edges and attach them to the front panel along with a paper tag and brad. Adhere a 5½" × 2½" [14cm × 6cm] piece of mesh to the inside panel. Cut around the word "work" on the patterned paper and adhere it as shown. Spell out the interior text with alphabet stickers and embellish with brads. Ink the edges of the card.

supplies • pink cardstock • black cardstock • white text-weight paper • black ink pad • 4 pink brads [Hot off the Press] • 4 pink silk flowers [Prima Marketing, Inc.] • 1 black silk flower [Prima Marketing, Inc.] • 3D-effect pens [Sakura of America] • font: Primer Print, Problem Secretary, TackODing [DaFont] • ruler • scissors or other cutting tool • bone folder [optional] • glue stick or other adhesive

Using a straight edge, cut the black cardstock into an arrow shape like the one shown here. Cut pink cardstock to 3⅞" × 7½" [10cm × 19cm]. Score and fold to create a 3¾" × 3⅞" [10cm × 10cm] card with the fold at the left, and adhere it to the front of the black arrow. Cut pink cardstock into a triangle slightly smaller than the top portion of the arrow, and adhere it as shown. Decorate the front of the card as shown with 3D-effect pens. Print the cover text on pink cardstock, cut to 3⅝" × 3⅝" [9cm × 9cm], ink the edges and adhere it to the front panel. Attach the silk flowers and brads to the front of the card. Print the interior text on text-weight paper, cut out each word and adhere them to the inside panel. Embellish with silk flowers.

supplies • blue cardstock [Bazzill Basics] • notebook-style patterned paper [Sassafrass Lass] • flowered paper [Sassafrass Lass] • light blue ink pad [Clearsnap] • text rub-on transfers [Mustard Moon] • assorted alphabet stickers [EK Success] • foam tape • sewing machine • white thread • ruler • scissors or other cutting tool • bone folder [optional] • glue stick or other adhesive

Linda Beeson

Cut cardstock to 5½" × 11" [14cm × 28cm]. Score and fold to create a 5½" × 5½" [14cm × 14cm] card with the fold at the top. Cut the notebook-style paper to 5¼" × 5¼" [13cm × 13cm], tear one edge and adhere it to the front panel. Apply the rub-on letters spelling "con-grats" to the flowered paper. Cut the "c," "o," "n" and "-" out separately. Cut "grats" out as one piece, cutting around one of the flowers on the patterned paper. Apply the remaining text to the front of the card using the alphabet stickers. Mount a flower from the patterned paper to the front of the card with a piece of foam tape. Cut a piece of the notebook-style patterned paper to 3½" × 2⅝" [9cm × 7cm] and tear one edge. Adhere this to the inside of the card and straight stitch along the torn edge. Spell out the interior text with stickers.

Caroline Ikeji

supplies

• turquoise cardstock • chevron-patterned paper [cherryArte, My Mind's Eye] • dotted paper [cherryArte, My Mind's Eye] • 2 matte silver brads [American Crafts] • 2 plastic flowers [Doodlebug Design, American Crafts] • fabric flower [Doodlebug Design, American Crafts] • 2 sticker strips [KI Memories] • alphabet epoxy stickers [KI Memories] • 2 journaling stickers [Heidi Swapp] • 2 1½" [4cm] pieces of decorative tape [Heidi Swapp] • black marker • red marker • black gel pen • paper clip [Magic Scraps] • sticky note • ruler • scissors or other cutting tool • bone folder [optional] • glue stick or other adhesive

Cut turquoise cardstock to 8½" × 5½" [22cm × 14cm]. Score and fold to create a 4¼" × 5½" [11cm × 14cm] card with the fold at the left. Adhere a 2" × 4½" [5cm × 11cm] piece of chevron-patterned paper to the front panel. Glue a 1" × 3" [3cm × 8cm] piece of dotted paper to the chevron-patterned paper. Handwrite the to-do list on the sticky note with the markers and pen and attach the paper clip. Attach the sticky note to the front panel. Adhere the journaling sticker and epoxy alphabet stickers as shown. Handwrite the cover text on the sticker strips and layer them over the journaling sticker. Embellish with the plastic flower, fabric flower and brad. Handwrite the interior text on a journaling sticker and apply it to the interior panel. Embellish with decorative tapes, a plastic flower and a brad.

supplies • black matchbook-style card [Die Cuts With a View] • green flowered paper [Mara-Mi, KI Memories] • orange flowered paper [Mara-Mi, KI Memories] • striped paper [Mara-Mi, KI Memories] • white text-weight paper • striped transparency [Tenika] • pink ink pad • text stickers [7gypsies] • chipboard star [Li'l Davis Designs] • 2 rhinestone stars • corner-rounder punch • font: Times New Roman • ruler • scissors or other cutting tool • bone folder [optional] • glue stick or other adhesive

Cut green flowered paper to 4" × 4" [10cm × 10cm], round two corners and adhere it to the long flap of the matchbook-style card. Adhere a ½" × 4¼" [1cm × 11cm] piece of striped paper to the short flap. Cut orange flowered paper to ½" × 4¼" [1cm × 11cm] and adhere it to the green flowered paper. Print the cover text on text-weight paper, trim and adhere it to the front of the card. Embellish with the text stickers, transparency strip and chipboard star as shown. Print the interior text on text-weight paper, trim into strips and ink the edges. Adhere the text strips and rhinestone stars to the inside panel.

Linda Beeson

supplies • white cardstock • scroll-patterned paper [BasicGrey] • red patterned paper [BasicGrey] • blue patterned paper [BasicGrey] • green ink pad • red ink pad • assorted alphabet rub-on transfers [All My Memories, Doodlebug Design] • rub-on transfer stitches [Die Cuts With a View] • alphabet stickers [Making Memories] • chipboard design [cherryArte] • corner-rounder punch • large scallop scissors • small scallop scissors • cleaning cloth • ruler • scissors or other cutting tool • bone folder [optional] • glue stick or other adhesive

Cut cardstock to 5½" × 11" [14cm × 28cm]. Score and fold to create a 5½" × 5½" [14cm × 14cm] card with the fold at the top. Ink the outside edges with green ink. Cut scroll-patterned paper to 5" × 4½" [13cm × 11cm]. Trim one short edge with large scallop scissors, round the remaining corners and adhere it to the front panel. Cut a 4½" × ⅝" [11cm × 2cm] strip of red paper and adhere it to the scroll-patterned paper. Prepare the chipboard design by applying green ink to the left side of the design and red ink to the right. Use the cleaning cloth to spread the green ink over the piece and to remove excess ink. Adhere the chipboard piece as shown. Apply the rub-on text and stitches as well as the alphabet stickers to the front of the card. Trim blue patterned paper to 4¾" × 4¾" [12cm × 12cm], round the corners and adhere it to the inside panel. Cut red paper to 5½" × ¾" [14cm × 2cm] with small scallop scissors and tear the short ends. Cut scroll-patterned paper to 5" × ½" [13cm × 1cm] and round two corners as shown. Layer these strips on the inside panel, then apply text and stitch rub-ons.

supplies • white cardstock • blue paper • black paper • pink paper • fashionable woman fabric [Michael Miller Memories] • alphabet stamps [Technique Tuesday] • black ink pad • black gel pen • pink photo corners [Heidi Swapp] • ruler • scissors or other cutting tool • bone folder [optional] • glue stick or other adhesive

Cut cardstock to 8½" × 11" [22cm × 28cm]. Score and fold to create a 5½" × 8½" [14cm × 22cm] card with the fold at the left. Ink the edges of a 4¼" × 5½" [11cm × 14cm] piece of blue paper and adhere it to the front panel. Cut a 3¼" × 6½" [8cm × 17cm] piece of fabric, adhere to white cardstock for stability and attach it to a 3¾" × 7" [10cm x 18cm] piece of black paper. Apply photo corners to the fabric and attach the black cardstock to the front panel. Stamp the cover text onto white cardstock and cut out each word. Ink the edges of the text blocks and adhere them with pink paper accents as shown. Cut a 4¼" × 5½" [11cm × 14cm] piece of blue paper and ink the edges. Handwrite the interior text on pink paper, trim it and ink the edges. Adhere the blue paper and the text to the inside panel.

Erin Edelmann

supplies • cream cardstock • light aqua cardstock • dotted paper [Junkitz] • vintage photo of a couple • text rub-on transfers [American Crafts] • alphabet tiles [Junkitz] • ruler • scissors or other cutting tool • bone folder [optional] • glue stick or other adhesive

Cut cream cardstock to 6" × 9" [15cm × 23cm]. Score and fold to create a 4½" × 6" [11cm × 15cm] card with the fold at the left. Cut light aqua cardstock to 3" × 4" [8cm × 10cm] and dotted paper to 2¾" × 3¾" [7cm x 10cm]. Layer the cardstock, dotted paper and couple image and adhere to the front of the card. Apply the rub-on transfers to spell out the text on the front and inside of the card as shown. Finish the interior sentiment by adhering alphabet tiles.

so i hear you got a

new boyfriend...

lucky

B I T C H

Christine Doyle

supplies • brown/flowered double-sided cardstock [My Mind's Eye] • brown ink pad • black pen • brown marker • chipboard letters [Li'l Davis Designs] • ruler • scissors or other cutting tool • bone folder [optional] • glue stick or other adhesive

Cut brown cardstock to 8½" × 5½" [22cm × 14cm]. Score and fold to create a 4½" × 5½" [11cm × 14cm] card with the fold at the top. Cut flowered paper to 4" × 5¾" [10cm × 15cm], ink the edges and adhere it off-center to the front of the card. Handwrite "lucky" in black ink and trace over the text with a brown marker. Attach the chipboard letters to the front of the card. [This card is blank inside.]

Surplus Sentiments

front   Happy birthday! You really don't look a day over 29.
inside   Lucky bitch.

front   I'd congratulate you on your engagement, but that huge rock on your hand is blinding me.
inside   Lucky bitch.

front   Heard you did well at the slots in Vegas!
inside   Lucky bitch.

front   I guess women like you are content to stay home and raise the kids.
inside   Lucky bitch.

front   I can't believe your superficial husband thinks plastic surgery is an acceptable anniversary gift.
inside   Lucky bitch!

front   To my only friend who can still shop in the juniors' section.
inside   Lucky bitch.

front   You think you can get away
with dressing like a teenager?
inside   Lucky bitch.

front   So you've gone from being
a small quesadilla to the big enchilada!
inside   Lucky bitch.

front   My deepest sympathies
on the loss of your mother-in-law.
inside   Lucky bitch.

front   Congratulation$ on
your divorce $ettlement.
inside   Lucky bitch.

front   Have so much
fun on your vacation!
inside   Lucky bitch!

front   After all these years,
it's become obvious that you
married for money.
inside   Lucky bitch.

front   Your mother-in-law is so nice!
inside   Lucky bitch!

front   Cheers to five years
of matrimonial bondage!
inside   Lucky bitch.

supplies • red cardstock • pink cardstock • dotted paper [Scenic Route Paper Co.] • black ink pad • rub-on transfers [BasicGrey] • alphabet stickers [Doodlebug Design] • metal alphabet pieces [Making Memories] • font: Bickley Script [Internet download] • ruler • scissors or other cutting tool • bone folder [optional] • glue stick or other adhesive

Score and fold an 8½" × 11" [22cm × 28cm] piece of red cardstock to form a card that is 8½" × 5½" [22cm × 14cm]. Freehand cut the card into the shape of a heart with the fold on the left. Trim pink cardstock and dotted paper to each fill half of the card front, leaving a small frame of red cardstock. Spell "anniversary" in alphabet stickers on red cardstock and trim around the letters. Ink the edges of this piece as well as the inside and outside edges of the card. Adhere the text strip to a larger piece of red cardstock and adhere to the front panel, trimming the edges of the text strip to fit the card. Print the interior text on pink cardstock, trim and adhere it to the inside panel.

I can't believe how long you've been making each other completely miserable!

supplies

• 5" × 7" [13cm x 18cm] file folder [DMD] • bull's eye-patterned paper [BasicGrey] • brown paper • flowered paper [BasicGrey] • time card patterned paper [Design Originals] • brown ink pad • alphabet stickers [Doodlebug Design] • chipboard piece [Technique Tuesday] • 9 red rhinestones • font: Dana [Internet download] • ruler • scissors or other cutting tool • bone folder [optional] • glue stick or other adhesive

NOW GET A JOB!

Linda Beeson

Using the file folder as a template, cut the bull's eye-patterned paper to fit the front panel and time-card-patterned paper to fit the right interior panel. Adhere each paper to its respective panel. Lightly ink both the inside and outside edges of the folder. Cut a flower from the flowered paper and adhere it to the front of the card. Glue the rhinestones to the center of the flower. Print the cover text on brown paper and trim it to fit the chipboard piece. Adhere the brown paper to the chipboard piece and adhere this to the front of the card. Spell the interior text with alphabet stickers.

Heidi Kinnamon

supplies

• textured white cardstock • smooth white cardstock • textured blue cardstock • black glossy paper • woman and frog prince stamp [Inky Antics] • black ink pad • 12" [30cm] gingham ribbon • variety of markers • 3D gloss medium [Ranger Industries] • glitter • hole punch • font: Bradley Hand ITC [Internet download] • ruler • scissors or other cutting tool • bone folder [optional] • glue stick or other adhesive

Cut white textured cardstock to 6¾" × 9½" [17cm × 24cm]. Score and fold to create a 4¾" × 6¾" [12cm × 17cm] card with the fold at the left. Print the cover text onto smooth white cardstock and trim to 3¾" × 4¾" [10cm × 12cm]. Stamp the woman and frog image onto this piece and color them with markers. Apply a coat of gloss medium, sprinkle on glitter, and allow the medium to dry. Layer the stamped piece, a 4" × 5" [10cm × 13cm] piece of the glossy black paper and a 4¼" × 6¼" [11cm × 16cm] piece of the textured blue cardstock. Punch 2 holes 2" [5cm] apart in the bottom of the blue cardstock, string the ribbon through the holes and tie into a bow. Adhere the blue cardstock to a 4½" × 6½" [11cm × 17cm] piece of black glossy paper. Glue the layered papers to the front of the card. Print the interior text on smooth white cardstock and cut to ½" × 2¼" [1cm × 6cm]. Mount the text on a ¾" × 2½" [2cm × 6cm] piece of textured blue cardstock and adhere it to the inside of the card.

You've got a date Saturday night!

I assume it's blind?

supplies • stitched cardstock [Sonburn] • blue card-stock • striped paper [Sonburn] • flowered paper [Sonburn] • green paper • brown ink pad • text rub-on transfers [Creative Imaginations, Doodlebug Design] • puppy clipart [Microsoft] • large chipboard flower [Maya Road] • small chipboard flower [Maya Road] • font: Century Bold [Microsoft] • ruler • scissors or other cutting tool • bone folder [optional] • glue stick or other adhesive

Too bad your dog is getting more action than you.

Alecia Ackerman Grimm

Cut stitched cardstock to 9" × 8½" [23cm × 22cm]. Score and fold to create a 4½" × 8½" [11cm × 22cm] card with the fold at the left. Cut striped paper to ½" × 4½" [1cm × 11cm] and adhere it to the front of the card. Ink the large chip-board flower with brown ink, attach flowered paper behind the opening and adhere it to the front of the card. Cover the small chipboard flower with green paper and adhere it to the large chipboard flower. Print out the puppy image, cut it out and adhere it to the small chipboard flower. Apply the text rub-ons to the front of the card. Print the interior text on blue cardstock, cut to 4½" × 8½" [11cm × 22cm] and adhere it to the inside of the card. Ink the card's edges.

Chapter 5

Just for [Poking] Fun

Some people give cards only on birthdays and holidays—but why wait for a special occasion when our *real* lives are happening every *other* day? This chapter is full of random fun that just about anyone can appreciate. But don't stop here. Once you start making greeting cards for nonoccasions, you'll realize noccasions occur all the time—and they deserve to be celebrated! Challenge yourself to create your own unique sentiments (or unsentiments) to make your friends' days. You'll show your friends that you care—and that you're there for them no matter what.

Stacey Stamitoles

supplies • blue cardstock • black cardstock • dotted paper [Bo-Bunny Press] • paisley-patterned paper [Bo-Bunny Press] • text rub-on transfers [K&Company, American Crafts, KI Memories] • scroll rub-on transfers [Prima Marketing, Inc.] • black paint pen • chipboard frame [Everlasting Keepsakes] • ruler • scissors or other cutting tool • bone folder [optional] • glue stick or other adhesive

Paint the chipboard frame with a black paint pen and allow to dry. Cut blue cardstock to 3⅞" × 7¾" [10cm × 20cm]. Score and fold to create a 3⅞" × 3⅞" [10cm × 10cm] card with the fold at the left. Adhere the card to the frame. Adhere the decorative papers to the front of the card in this order: a ⅞" × 3⅞" [2cm × 10cm] piece of blue cardstock on a 1" × 3⅞" [3cm × 10cm] piece of black cardstock on a 2¼" × 3⅞" [6cm × 10cm] piece of paisley-patterned paper on a 3¼" × 3⅞" [8cm × 10cm] piece of dotted paper. Apply the text and scroll rub-ons to the front panel. Adhere a 3½" × 3½" [9cm × 9cm] piece of dotted paper to the inside panel and apply the rub-on text.

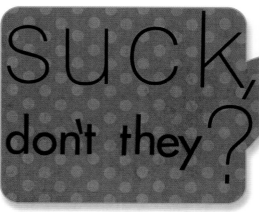

supplies • teal double-sided cardstock [WorldWin Papers] • denim-patterned paper [Cloud 9 Design] • flowered paper [Cloud 9 Design] • cream cardstock • text rub-on transfers [Wordsworth] • 2 chipboard paisley pieces [Cloud 9 Design] • small scallop scissors • font: Still Time [Internet download] • sewing machine • white thread • ruler • scissors or other cutting tool • bone folder [optional] • glue stick or other adhesive

Linda Beeson

Cut teal cardstock to 5½" × 11" [14cm × 28cm]. Score and fold to create a 5½" × 5½" [14cm × 14cm] card with the fold at the left. Trim denim-patterned paper to 5¼" × 5¼" [13cm × 13cm] and adhere it to the front panel. Cut 4 strips from the flowered paper to 1" × 12" [3cm × 30cm], pleat the strips and straight stitch them to the front of the card. Print the cover text on cream cardstock, trim, frame with a slightly larger piece of teal cardstock, and adhere it to the front panel. Embellish with the larger chipboard piece. Cut denim-patterned paper to 5¼" × 5¼" [13cm × 13cm] with scalloped scissors and adhere it to the inside panel. Apply the rub-on text to the denim-patterned paper. Cut thin strips of the flowered paper and use them to frame the interior text. Embellish with the remaining chipboard piece.

Caroline Ikeji

supplies • orange cardstock • yellow cardstock • striped paper [Urban Lily, Provo Craft] • dotted paper [Urban Lily, Provo Craft] • solid pink paper • note paper [Junkitz] • black ink pad • text rub-on transfers [American Crafts] • transparent flower [Heidi Swapp] • alphabet stickers [American Crafts] • pencil • flower clip [Making Memories] • 3 rhinestone flowers [Heidi Swapp] • chipboard accent [EK Success] • ruler • scissors or other cutting tool • bone folder [optional] • glue stick or other adhesive

Cut orange cardstock to 8½" × 5½" [22cm × 14cm]. Score and fold to create a 4¼" × 5½" [11cm × 14cm] card with the fold at the left. Layer the following papers on the front panel in this order: 1¼" × 4¼" [3cm × 11cm] striped paper with inked edges and a torn edge, 2½" × 4¼" [6cm × 11cm] dotted paper with inked edges, 2½" × 3½" [6cm × 8cm] yellow cardstock with inked edges, 3½" × 1½" [8cm × 4cm] note paper with inked edges. Embellish with the transparent flower, chipboard piece and rhinestone flowers as shown. Apply the rub-on text to pink paper, trim and adhere it to the front of the card. Use alphabet stickers to spell "lovely" on the note paper. Use alphabet stickers and handwriting to spell the interior text on yellow cardstock, trim and adhere to the inside panel.

NOT

supplies • white cardstock • circle-patterned paper [BasicGrey, KI Memories] • vine-patterned paper [BasicGrey, KI Memories] • dotted paper [BasicGrey, KI Memories] • red paper [BasicGrey, KI Memories] • newsprint stamp [Stampers Anonymous] • red ink pad • corner-rounder punch • font: Arial [Microsoft] • ruler • scissors or other cutting tool • bone folder [optional] • glue stick or other adhesive

Cut white cardstock to 7½" × 6" [19cm × 15cm]. Score and fold at 3" [8cm] so the front panel is longer than the back, with the fold at the top. Adhere a 7½" × 6" [19cm × 15cm] piece of circle-patterned paper to the inside panel. Stamp the front panel with the newsprint stamp and scallop the bottom edge using the corner punch. Trim circle-patterned paper to 3" × 6" [8cm × 15cm] and adhere it to the front panel, along with a 2¼" × 3" [6cm × 8cm] piece of vine-patterned paper. Print the cover text on dotted paper, trim and adhere it as shown. Embellish with 3" [8cm] strips of red paper. Print the interior text on dotted paper, trim to 1¼" × 6" [3cm × 15cm] and adhere it to the inside panel, along with a 2¼" × 6" [6cm × 15cm] piece of vine-patterned paper.

supplies • tag and pocket card [Making Memories] • white cardstock • alphabet stamps [Provo Craft] • black ink pad • 7" [18cm] piece of blue ribbon • assortment of blue buttons • scissors or other cutting tool • glue stick or other adhesive

Stamp the cover text onto white cardstock and cut out each word. Attach the words and buttons to the outside of the card pocket. Stamp the interior text on the tag and attach the ribbon.

STOP
DUCKING

supplies
• textured white cardstock • harlequin-patterned paper [Imaginisce] • flowered/checkered double-sided paper [Imaginisce] • white text-weight paper • rub-on transfer images [Imaginisce] • 3 assorted rhinestone flowers [Imaginisce] • font: CK Cosmopolitan [Creating Keepsakes] • pencil • sewing machine • white thread • craft knife • cutting mat • ruler • scissors or other cutting tool • bone folder [optional] • glue stick or other adhesive

Print the text on white cardstock, cut to 8" × 8" [20cm × 20cm], and score and fold to create a 4" × 8" [10cm × 20cm] card with the fold at the left and the text on the right interior panel. Cut teal paper to 3¾" × 8" [10cm × 20 cm] and adhere it to the front panel. Cut double-sided paper to 3½" × 8" [9cm × 20cm] and zigzag stitch it [flowered-side-up] to the card as shown. Cut another piece of double-sided paper to 4" × 3¼" [10cm × 8cm] and attach it [checkered-side-up] with zigzag stitches as shown. Cut a window in the front panel with the craft knife to reveal the words "Let's Do Lunch." Embellish with rhinestone flowers. Cut double-sided paper to 2¼" × ⅝" [6cm × 2cm] and adhere it under the interior sentiment along with rub-on transfers as shown.

('Cause it's your turn to pay.)

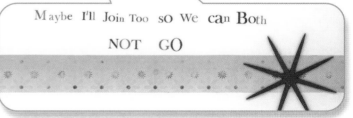

Maybe I'll Join Too so We can Both

NOT GO

supplies • white cardstock • flowered paper [Around the Block] • brown ink antiquing tool [Around the Block] • text rub-on transfers [Heidi Grace Designs] • chipboard circle border [Majestic Memories] • chipboard star • flower punch [Fiskars] • ruler • scissors or other cutting tool • bone folder [optional] • glue stick or other adhesive

Cut white cardstock to 8¼" × 8½" [21cm × 22cm]. Score and fold at 4¼" [11cm], with the fold at the top, so the front panel is shorter than the back. Ink the edges with the antiquing tool. Cut flowered paper to 3¾" × 8¼" [10cm × 21cm] and adhere it to the front panel. Punch the remainder of the flowered paper five times with the flower punch. Ink the chipboard border with the antiquing tool, attach it to the bottom front edge of the card as shown, then adhere several of the punched-out flowers as shown. Apply text rub-ons to the front and inside of the card. Adhere a ⅞" × 8½" [2cm × 22cm] strip of flowered paper to the inside panel beneath the text. Ink the chipboard flower with the antiquing tool and adhere it as shown.

Heather D. White

supplies • circle-patterned/rust double-sided paper [We R Memory Keepers] • cream lace-patterned paper [We R Memory Keepers] • 3 coordinating patterned papers [We R Memory Keepers] • brown ink pad • bronze-colored mini brad [All My Memories] • font: CK Lazy Days [Creating Keepsakes] • dumbbell template [see page 106] • ruler • scissors or other cutting tool • bone folder [optional] • glue stick or other adhesive

Cut double-sided paper to 7" × 6½" [18cm × 17cm]. Score and fold to create a 3½" × 6½" [9cm × 17cm] card with the fold at the top. Print the cover text on cream paper and trim to 3" × 6" [8cm × 15cm]. Using the dumbbell template, cut out dumbbell pieces from three coordinating patterned papers. Lightly ink the edges of the dumbbell pieces, the cream paper and the card. Attach the dumbbell pieces to the cream paper as shown and adhere this piece to the front panel. Print the interior text on cream paper, trim to ¾" × 3" [2cm × 8cm], lightly ink the edges and adhere it to the inside panel. Embellish with the brad.

supplies • brown cardstock • teal cardstock • flowered paper [Around the Block] • flower stamp [See Dee's Stamps] • pink ink pad • black ink pad • rub-on transfer images [BasicGrey] • metal house token [Colorbök] • rain dots [Cloud 9 Design] • chipboard frame [Trace Industries] • ruler • scissors or other cutting tool • bone folder [optional] • glue stick or other adhesive

Cut brown cardstock to 8¼" × 9½" [21cm × 24cm]. Score and fold to create a 4⅛" × 9½" [10cm × 24cm] card with the fold at the left. Print the cover text on flowered paper, aligning the text to fit the windows in the chipboard frame. Cut around the first and last lines of text and adhere them to the frame. Adhere the remaining text to the front of the card where the frame's openings will be, then add the rub-ons and inked house token. Stamp the frame as shown. Adhere it to the front of the card, and adhere a 2¼" × 4" [6cm × 10cm] piece of teal cardstock to the inside. Print the interior text on flowered paper, trim and adhere it as shown. Embellish with rain dots.

You've got it all:

The perfect job,

The perfect house,

And now

The perfect man.

I am so happy for you!

Seriously,

These are tears of joy.

supplies • brown cardstock • striped paper [Paper Salon] • heart-patterned paper [Paper Salon] • scroll-patterned paper [Paper Salon] • news flash tag [7gypsies] • text rub-on transfers [U.S Stamp & Sign] • 6 brown brads [Miss Elizabeth's] • zigzag scissors • font: Arial Rounded [Microsoft] • sewing machine • brown thread • ruler • scissors or other cutting tool • bone folder [optional] • glue stick or other adhesive

Cut brown cardstock to 7½" × 7¼" [19cm × 18cm]. Score and fold to create a 3¾" × 7¼" [10cm × 18cm] card with the fold at the left. Cut the three patterned papers to 7" × 3½" [18cm × 9cm]. Tear the short edges of the scroll-patterned paper and straight stitch it to the striped paper. Repeat with the heart-patterned paper, then adhere the papers to the front panel. Embellish with brads. Apply rub-ons to the tag, adhere it as shown, and zigzag stitch along one side. Print the interior text on heart-patterned paper, cut to 7" × 3½" [18cm × 9cm], trim one long edge with zigzag scissors and adhere it to the inside panel. Tear a 7" [18cm] strip of scroll-patterned paper and straight stitch it to the edge of the heart-patterned paper.

Linda Beeson

supplies • green cardstock • pink cardstock • striped paper [KI Memories] • book pocket [Boxer Scrapbook Productions] • 3 coordinating paper tags [KI Memories] • 1 orange brad [Making Memories] • alphabet, punctuation and flower stickers [KI Memories] • 3 9" [23cm] pieces of assorted ribbon [Berwick Offray] • circle hole punch • font: Journaling Hand [Typadelic] • ruler • scissors or other cutting tool • glue stick or other adhesive

Cut green cardstock to 3¼" × 4½" [8cm × 11cm], striped paper to 3" × 4¼" [8cm × 11cm] and pink cardstock to 2½" × 3¾" [6cm × 10cm]. Adhere these papers to one another as shown and add the small tag to the top edge. Print "I heard you were looking for" and "Isn't your boyfriend enough" on pink cardstock in separate blocks. Cut the interior text into a circle, adhere it to a larger circle cut from green cardstock, and attach this to the inside panel, along with the question mark and flower sticker. Adhere ribbons around the book pocket. Cut out the cover text, adhere it to the text tag, and attach this to the front panel. Apply the stickers spelling "work," the flower sticker and the brad to the remaining tag and adhere it as shown.

sometimes I look at you

And find myself thinking

How courageous you are.

I would not be caught

dead in that outfit.

Kelly Anne Grundhauser

supplies • red cardstock • striped paper [All My Memories] • flowered paper [All My Memories] • printable cotton [Shortcuts!] • assorted flower stamps [See Dee's Stamps] • yellow ink pad • pink ink pad • die-cut flowers [All My Memories] • font: Jenkins v2.0 [Internet download] • white thread • sewing machine • ruler • scissors or other cutting tool • bone folder [optional] • glue stick or other adhesive

Cut red cardstock to 7" × 8¾" [18cm × 22cm]. Score and fold at 4¼" [11cm] with the fold at the top, so the front panel is shorter than the back. Cut striped paper to 4" × 6¾" [10cm × 17cm] and adhere it to the front panel. Cut flowered paper to 2¾" × 6¾" [7cm × 17cm] and cut to form a wave. Adhere the flowered paper as shown and zigzag stitch along its top edge. Print the cover text on printable cotton, cut it into strips, and adhere them to the front panel. Embellish with die-cut flowers. Cut a 2½" × 3" [6cm × 8cm] piece of flowered paper and cut the top edge into a curve. Attach it to the inside panel with zigzag stitch. Print the interior text on printable cotton, trim, adhere the sentiment and stamp it as shown. Ink the card's edges.

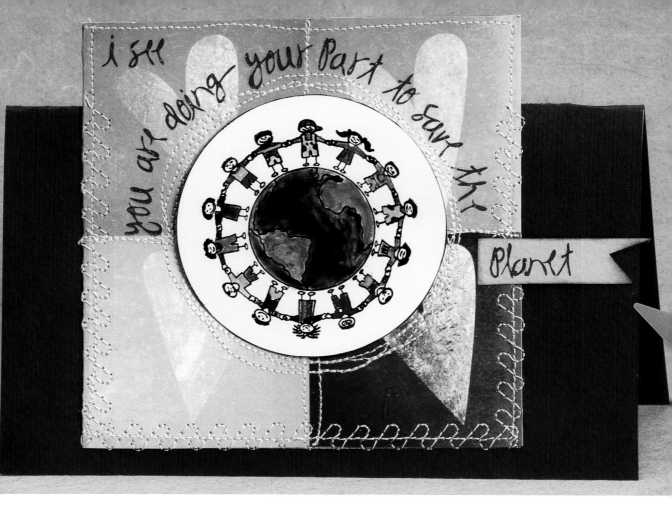

supplies • brown cardstock • light blue cardstock • glossy white cardstock • heart-patterned paper [Around the Block] • label-patterned paper [Calambour] • planet stamp [Rubber Stampede] • black ink pad • brown ink pad • text rub-on transfers [Li'l Davis Designs] • rub-on recycling symbol [BasicGrey] • shimmering watercolor cakes [Luminarte] • magnet • clear plastic cups • unused film strip • wine bottle hole punch [Marvy Uchida] • white thread • sewing machine • ruler • scissors or other cutting tool • bone folder [optional] • glue stick or other adhesive

Cut brown cardstock to 7" × 8½" [18cm × 20cm]. Score and fold to create a 4¼" × 7" [11cm × 18cm] card with the fold at the top. Cut heart-patterned paper to 4¾" × 4¾" [12cm × 12cm] and stitch the paper as shown. Add text rub-ons, then adhere the heart-patterned paper to the front of the card. Apply the remaining rub-on text to light blue cardstock, trim around the text as shown, ink the edges and adhere it to the front panel. Stamp the globe image onto glossy cardstock, color it with watercolors and cut around the image. Attach a magnet to the back of the

stamped piece and adhere it to the front of the card with a glue dot. [The stamped piece may be removed and used as a magnet.] Cut label-patterned paper to 4¼" × 7" [11cm × 18cm] and adhere it to the inside panel. Cut blue cardstock into two pieces that form the shape of the recycling bin. Apply the rub-on symbol to the cardstock. Cut several wine bottles from plastic cups and the film strip, adding labels to some from the label-patterned paper. Adhere the bottles and recycling bin to the inside of the card.

Basic Card-Making Materials

It doesn't take much to get started making greeting cards. One trip through the house collecting the art supplies you have and a quick trip to the local craft, stamp or scrapbook store should produce all the materials you need. If you're unfamiliar with the supplies used in this book, this is a good summary of everything you need.

Paper

There are two kinds of paper used predominantly in card making. Cardstock is a heavyweight paper often used as the base of a card. Cardstock is available in solid colors, with or without texture, as well as in patterned designs.

Patterned paper is as heavy as good copier paper. It can be used in small sections as an accent to your design, or to cover the entire front or inside of the card. If you haven't been to a scrapbook or craft store lately, you won't believe the variety of patterned papers available.

Cutting Tools

Scissors can always be used to cut paper, but there are other tools available that are even easier to use. Slide paper trimmers, found at craft and scrapbook stores, make quick work of cutting straight lines. Many are large enough to accommodate 12" x 12" [30cm × 30cm] sheets of paper, and some come with a scoring blade.

Another option for cutting straight lines is to use a craft knife, metal-edged ruler and cutting mat. The ruler allows you to guide the knife with the straight edge, and the mat protects your work surface.

Once you get beyond straight lines, you'll find that small detail scissors come in handy. These allow you to trim neatly around a flower on a piece of patterned paper or to cut a simple wavy line.

Shape cutters and paper punches allow you to cut smooth-edged shapes in a snap. Shape cutters come with special cutting tools and templates. For smaller shapes, a paper punch works well.

Adhesives

There are a ton of adhesives available, many that work best in specific situations. If you're just getting started, all you need is a glue stick or double-sided tape for attaching paper to paper, and craft glue or glue dots for attaching heavier or more dimensional items to paper.

Stamping Supplies

Rubber stamps and ink pads are terrific tools for adding images and color to your cards. Rubber stamps of every kind are available at craft, scrapbook and stamping stores.

The type of ink pad you use can matter in some instances. If you're stamping on something other than paper or if you'll be coloring in the image with watercolors, use a permanent ink pad. If you want to emboss a stamped image with embossing powder, use a pigment ink pad. In most other cases, however, either of these types or a dye ink pad will do the trick.

Adding color to stamped images is fun and can be done with colored pencils, watercolor pencils, markers—whatever suits your fancy.

Continue on through the next few pages to see some of these supplies, and more, in action!

Simple Papercrafting Techniques

With just a few easy techniques, you'll be making these cards and other sassy creations of your own in no time.

Scoring and Folding a Card

Premade card bases are readily available at craft, stamp and scrapbook stores, but if you don't mind making your own, you'll find your card base options will grow exponentially.

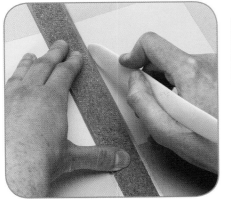 

1. To score a card, measure to find the center (or the desired location for your fold) and make marks at this point at the top and bottom of the card. Line a ruler up on the marks, and score the line by running a bone folder along the ruler from top to bottom.

2. Fold the card along the score line, then use the bone folder again to burnish the fold, making the crease nice and crisp.

Punching out Shapes

Paper punches make cutting out small shapes easy. A collection of a few geometric-shaped stamps and maybe a flower punch or two will add much to your card creations. Should your punches ever get dull, simply punch a piece of aluminum foil a few times to sharpen the blade.

To use a paper punch on solid paper, simply place the punch flat on your work surface and punch away. If, however, you want to punch a specific area out of patterned paper, turn the punch over to find the right spot. Then punch by pressing the punch side on the work surface [if you're really talented] or hold the paper in place, turn the punch over and punch as normal.

Using Rub-On Transfers

Rub-on transfers come in sheets, like stickers, but when they're transferred onto your card's surface, the effect is a clean, seamless look.

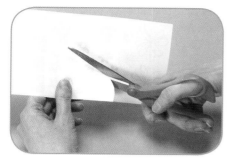

1. With scissors, cut out the image or word you want to transfer.

2. Remove the white paper backing, and place the image onto the paper. Using either the stick that comes with the rub-ons or a bone folder, rub the plastic side, making sure to rub over every part of the image.

3. Slowly peel the plastic off to reveal the transfer. If any part of the image isn't completely transferred, simply press the plastic back down and rub over it again.

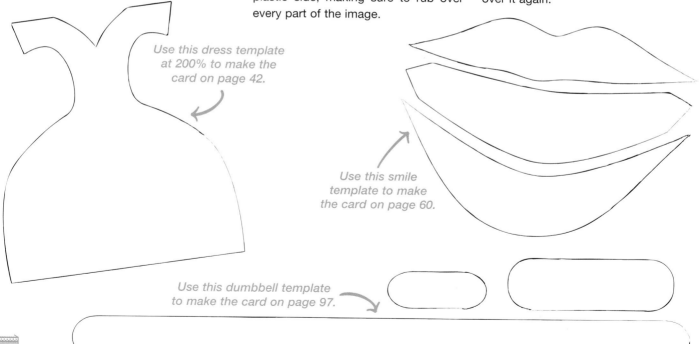

Use this dress template at 200% to make the card on page 42.

Use this smile template to make the card on page 60.

Use this dumbbell template to make the card on page 97.

Stamping a Rubber Stamp

Rubber stamps are quick and easy tools for transferring just the right image or sentiment onto your cards. No special skills are needed, but the following pointers will make the process go a bit smoother.

1. Lightly tap the stamp onto the ink pad. Pressing the stamp into the pad can overink the stamp and result in a messy image.

2. Press the stamp firmly onto the paper, or whatever you're stamping. It sometimes helps to stand as you press. Rocking the stamp as you press, though, will result in a smeared image.

3. Lift the stamp up and away to reveal the image.

Tip: *If you're stamping a large image or if you want to ink only part of a stamp, turn the stamp over and tap the pad onto the rubber.*

Using a Sewing Machine

Adding a little sewing to cards isn't hard. Whether you purchase a small craft sewing machine or use your mother's old hand-me-down, you will find that sewing a few simple stitches can really add a lot of character to your paper projects. All you need to do is take a few moments to read the instructions for your machine—at least how to thread the needle and bobbin—and have fun playing!

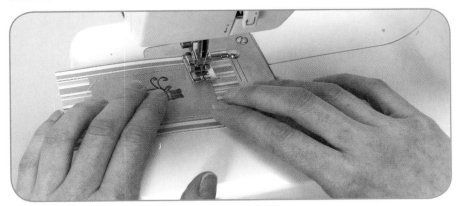

Feed the paper, or fabric, slowly as you sew—this helps you to maintain control of where you're sewing. For straight lines, use the edge of the presser foot or guidelines to the right of the presser foot to help you along.

Use this heart template at 200% to make the card on page 67.

Adding Color to a Stamped Image

Once your image is stamped, you can use it as is or add a bit of color to it. Coloring in a stamp will bring back fond memories of your favorite coloring books, but with a slightly more sophisticated look. Colored pencils, markers, watercolor pencils or regular watercolors are just a few of the tools you can use.

When using colored pencils to color a stamp, a dull tip will give you a softer look than a sharpened tip. You can also rub your finger over the colored image to soften it a bit more.

Inking Paper Edges

Whether a piece of cut paper is stamped or not, you may want to ink the edges to give it a special effect. To soften the edges of the paper to help it blend into the rest of your design, use an ink color similar to the paper in your design. To make a piece of paper stand out, on the other hand, ink the edges with a contrasting color.

To ink the edges of a piece of paper, lightly tap the edges onto an ink pad. If you'd like a little more of the color on the front of the paper, press a little harder into the ink pad.

For a lot of color on the front of the paper, smear the paper with the ink pad. Use a light hand and gradually add more color until you create your desired effect.

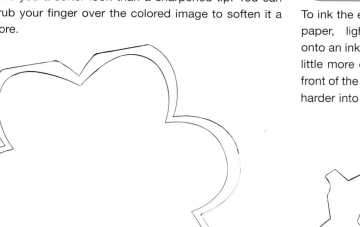

Use these flower templates at 200% to make the card on page 59.

Use this lemon template to make the card on pages 12–13.

Use this dress template at 200% to make the card on page 43.

Resources

The products used in this book can be found at your local scrapbook, rubber stamp or craft store. If you aren't able to find a particular product, contact the manufacturer listed below for a retailer in your area.

7gypsies
877-749-7797
www.sevengypsies.com

Abstract Fonts
www.abstractfonts.com

All My Memories
888-553-1998
www.allmymemories.com

American Crafts
801-226-0747
www.americancrafts.com

American Greetings
www.americangreetings.com

Around the Block
801-593-1946
www.aroundtheblockproducts.com

Art Gone Wild
800-945-3980
www.agwstamps.com

Autumn Leaves
800-588-6707
www.autumnleaves.com

BasicGrey
801-544-1116
www.basicgrey.com

Bazzill Basics Paper
480-558-8557
www.bazzillbasics.com

Berwick Offray, LLC
800-BERWICK
www.offray.com

Bo-Bunny Press
801-771-4010
www.bobunny.com

Boxer Scrapbook
Productions, LLC
888-625-6255
www.boxerscrapbooks.com

Cactus Pink
866-798-2446
www.cactuspink.com

Calambour
www.calambour.it

Carson-Dellosa
Publishing Co., Inc.
800-321-0943
www.carsondellosa.com

Cartwrights's Glitter
www.ccartwright.com

Chatterbox, Inc.
888-416-6260
www.chatterboxinc.com

cherryArte
212-465-3495
www.cherryarte.com

Clearsnap, Inc.
888-448-4862
www.clearsnap.com

Cloud 9 Design
866-348-5661
www.cloud9design.biz

Colorbök, Inc.
800-366-4660
www.colorbok.com

Crate Paper
702-966-0409
www.cratepaper.com

Creating Keepsakes
888-247-5282
www.creatingkeepsakes.com

Creative Imaginations
800-942-6487
www.cigift.com

Creative Memories
800-468-9335
www.creativememories.com

DaFont
www.dafont.com

Daisy Bucket Designs
541-289-3299
www.daisybucketdesigns.com

Design Originals
www.d-originals.com

Die Cuts With a View
801-224-6766
www.diecutswithaview.com

Doodlebug Design Inc.
877-800-9190
www.doodlebug.ws

EK Success, Ltd.
800-524-1349
www.eksuccess.com

Everlasting Keepsakes
816-896-7037
www.everlastingkeepsakes.com

Fancy Pants Designs, LLC
801-779-3212
www.fancypantsdesigns.com

Fiskars
866-348-5661
www.fiskars.com

Flair Designs
888-546-9990
www.flairdesignsinc.com

fontwerks
604-942-3105
www.fontwerks.com

Hambly Screen Prints
408-496-1100
www.hamblyscreenprints.com

Hampton Art
800-229-1019
www.hamptonart.com

Heidi Grace Designs, Inc.
866-348-5661
www.heidigrace.com

Heidi Swapp/Advantus
Corporation
904-482-0092
www.heidiswapp.com

Hot off the Press, Inc.
800-227-9595
www.b2b.hotp.com

Imaginisce
801-908-8111
www.imaginisce.com

Inky Antics Rubber Stamps
www.inkyantics.com

JoAnn Stores
www.joann.com

Junkitz
732-792-1108
www.junkitz.com

K&Company, LLC
888-244-2083
www.kandcompany.com

Karen Foster Design
801-451-9779
www.karenfosterdesign.com

KI Memories
972-243-5595
www.kimemories.com

Li'l Davis Designs
www.lildavisdesigns.com

Luminarte
866-229-1544
www.luminarteinc.com

Magic Mesh
651-345-6374
www.magicmesh.com

Making Memories
801-294-0430
www.makingmemories.com

Mara-Mi, Inc.
800-627-2648
www.mara-mi.com

Marvy Uchida/Uchida
of America, Corp.
800-541-5877
www.uchida.com

May Arts
800-442-3950
www.mayarts.com

Maya Road, LLC
877-427-7764
www.mayaroad.com

Memories Complete, LLC
866-966-6365
www.memoriescomplete.com

Michael Miller Memories
646-230-8862
www.michaelmillermemories.com

Mom's Corner for Kids
www.momscorner4kids.com

Mustard Moon
763-493-5157
www.mustardmoon.com

My Mind's Eye, Inc.
800-665-5116
www.mymindseye.com

NRN Designs
888-678-2734
www.nrndesigns.com

paper candy
800-311-9757
www.papercandy.com

Paper Salon
800-627-2648
www.papersalon.com

Pink Martini Designs, LLC
845-228-5833
www.pinkmartinidesigns.com

Plaid Enterprises, Inc.
800-842-4197
www.plaidonline.com

Polar Bear Press
801-451-7670
www.polarbearpress.com

Prima Marketing, Inc.
909-627-5532
www.primamarketinginc.com

Prism Papers
866-902-1002
www.prismpapers.com

Provo Craft and Novelty, Inc.
800-937-7686
www.provocraft.com

PSX Design
www.sierra-enterprises.com/
psxmain.html

Queen & Co.
858-613-7858
www.queenandcompany.com

Ranger Industries, Inc.
732-389-3535
www.rangerink.com

Rubber Stampede
800-423-4135
www.rubberstampede.com

Sakura of America
800-776-6257
www.sakuraofamerica.com

Sassafras Lass
801-269-1331
www.sassafraslass.com

Scenic Route Paper Co.
801-225-5754
www.scenicroutepaper.com

Scrapworks/As You
Wish Products, LLC
801-363-1010
www.scrapworks.com

SEI, Inc.
800-333-3279
www.shopsei.com

Sonburn
800-436-4919
www.sonburn.com

Stampers Anonymous
800-945-3980
www.stampersanonymous.com

Stampin' Up!
800-782-6787
www.stampinup.com

Technique Tuesday, LLC
503-644-4073
www.techniquetuesday.com

Tenika
www.tenika.com

Trace Industries, LLC
201-767-5696
www.traceind.com

Two Peas in a Bucket
888-896-7327
www.twopeasinabucket.com

Typadelic
www.typadelic.com

Urban Lily
www.urbanlily.com

U.S. Stamp & Sign
800-347-1044
www.usstamp.com

USArtQuest, Inc.
517-522-6225
www.usartquest.com

We R Memory Keepers, Inc.
801-539-5000
www.weronthenet.com

Wordsworth
877-280-0934
www.wordsworthstamps.com

WorldWin Papers
888-843-6455
www.worldwinpapers.com

Zsiage, LLC
718-224-1976
www.zsiage.com

Index

Index of Contributing Designers

Check out these other sassy selections from North Light Books!

Girlfriend Greetings
Edited by Christine Doyle

Girlfriend Greetings is filled with cards that help girlfriends celebrate each other. Inside you'll find 60 simple and stylish cards to give to your friends for every occasion, including celebratory greetings for birthdays and new jobs, and even consolation cards for nasty breakups and bad haircuts. You'll also get cheeky sidebars and technique tips. All crafting skill levels will find success with this book.

ISBN-13: 978-1-58180-862-9
ISBN-10: 1-58180-862-3
paperback, 96 pages, Z0274

Paper Every Day
Laurie Dewberry

Scrapbook materials aren't just for scrapbooks anymore. If you've fallen for the gorgeous patterned papers lining craft-store aisles, you'll love the projects in this book that show you how to put those materials to use in exciting new ways. Choose from 30 simple and savvy projects to enrich your everyday life or to make special occasions more memorable. Projects include everything from calendars to keepsake boxes and family storybooks.

ISBN-13: 978-1-58180-840-7
ISBN-10: 1-58180-840-2
paperback, 128 pages, Z0009

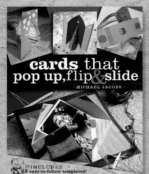

Cards That Pop-Up, Flip & Slide
Michael Jacobs

In this creative guide to making dynamic, interactive cards, you'll learn how to craft one-of-a-kind greetings with moving parts such as pop-ups, sliders and flaps. Choose from 22 step-by-step projects that use a variety of papers—from handmade and printed to recycled—to create unique graphic looks. You'll also learn how to create coordinating envelopes to complete the look of your cards. You'll be inspired to jazz up all of your cards with the fun and easy techniques in this book, including using inks, collage and colored pencils in fresh new ways.

ISBN-13: 978-1-58180-596-3
ISBN-10: 1-58180-596-9
paperback, 96 pages, 33109

Imperfect Lives
Laura Solomon and Tara Governo

This book celebrates scrapbookers who have the courage to tackle the real-life situations that have made them grow as people and artists. *Imperfect Lives* is for crafters who want to creatively scrapbook the realities of life including motherhood, the hard work of marriage, the heartbreak of divorce and the challenges of aging. Inside, readers will discover a wide range of trendsetting, artistic styles that exemplify the whole range of life experience. With pages that capture stories and circumstances ranging from profound and compelling to edgy and honest, *Imperfect Lives* revolutionizes the art of scrapbooking.

ISBN-13: 978-1-892127-94-5
ISBN-10: 1-892127-94-6
paperback, 128 pages, Z0531

These books and other fine North Light titles are available at your local craft or scrapbook store, bookstore or from online suppliers.